THE
POCKET GUIDE
TO

THE
POCKET GUIDE
TO

BART KING

GIBBS SMITH
TO ENRICH AND INSPIRE HUMANKIND
Salt Lake City | Charleston | Santa Fe | Santa Barbara

First Edition
12 11 10 09 08   5 4 3 2 1

This book makes mention of some activities that theoretically
could carry an element of risk. Readers assume all legal
responsibility for their actions.

Please contact the author at *kingbart@comcast.net*.

Published by
Gibbs Smith
P.O. Box 667
Layton, Utah 84041

Orders: 1.800.835.4993
www.gibbs-smith.com

Designed by Michel Vrána, Black Eye Design
Printed and bound in Canada

Library of Congress Cataloging-in-Publication Data

Pocket guide to games / edited by Bart King. – 1st ed.
    p. cm.
 ISBN-13: 978-1-4236-0469-3
 ISBN-10: 1-4236-0469-5
1. Games. 2. Amusements. 3. Sports for children. I. King,
    Bart, 1962-
GV1203.P63 2008
790.15–dc22

                        2008006907

To anyone who's ever accidentally scored on his or her own team! (You're not alone.)

★★★

Many of the games in this book were originally published in *Games for the Playground, Home, School and Gymnasium* by Jessie H. Bancroft, © 1909 by The Macmillan Company, and have been updated here for modern-day use. Other games are original contributions of the author, though forms of the games might be played throughout the world with similar or varying rules, strategies and names.

In addition, I offer my grateful appreciation to the following people, who suggestions and resourcefulness enriched this book: Kelly Mucha, Marie Constant, Jerry Christiansen, Janice Johnson, Lilian McConville, Carlyle Krohn, Brody vander-Sommen, Madge Baird, and Suzanne Taylor.

"ONE DARES TO HOPE THAT THIS LITTLE CRAFT, BEARING AS IT DOES SUCH A FREIGHT OF GLADNESS, MAY LEAVE BEHIND A WAKE OF CHEER, AND LAUGHTER, AND HAPPINESS."

—JESSIE H. BANCROFT 1869–1952

CONTENTS

★★★

Introduction

Games for the Playground, Home, School and Gymnasium

My face hurt every Friday morning.

This is not a set-up for a bad joke.[1] If you've ever grinned for a long period of time, you know that facial muscles can cramp up painfully. And one day a week, *my* mug convulsed during my homeroom period. Monday through Thursday mornings I provided academic tutoring for my seventh graders, but Friday was *Game*

---

1. *"Does your face hurt? Because it's killing me."*

Day. That's when my class would stampede down to the Fitness Room and the questions would start.

"WHAT ARE WE PLAYING TODAY? HOGIE BALL? CAN WE PLAY HOGIE BALL AGAIN?"

"CAN'T WE DO QUADRANT HOCKEY THIS TIME?"

"WHY DON'T WE HAVE ANOTHER TROLL WAR TOURNAMENT?"

The Fitness Room was an oversized space, outfitted with everything a game lover could want. There was a climbing wall, a climbing net, a padded floor mat, an assortment of balls, and cones galore. We could compete individually, in small groups, or (best of all) in full-class contests with rival homerooms.

This gaming laboratory inspired my colleagues and me to invent and hybridize new games, and so Silent Ball, Mongol Ball, Odd Ball, Paranoia Ball, and the dreaded Hogie Ball were born. Watching the results did more than make our faces cramp up; in addition to enjoying belly laughs, we all learned important lessons about life, the world, and ourselves.[2]

But when Friday rolled around, there was also a lot of pressure to come up with a new game, and my job would have been much easier if I'd known about Jessie H. Bancroft's 1909 book *Games for the Playground, Home, School and Gymnasium*. Upon its publication, the *New York Times* lauded the book as "a valuable and beneficent service for humanity," and if that seems like remarkable praise, well, Jessie Hubbell Bancroft was a remarkable woman.

Born in 1869, Bancroft grew up a gifted but sickly child in Minnesota. Her frailty gave her a sensible interest in all matters healthy, and as a young woman, she studied nutrition and exercise at Cambridge and Harvard. Bancroft

---

2. *For a full list of life lessons, talk to your mother.*

lectured widely, and she achieved fame for her dynamic presentations and ready wit. Although most women of her time didn't finish high school, Ms. Bancroft became a Columbia professor. Just as remarkably, she apparently overcame her ill health through exercise and willpower; a journalist noted Bancroft's successes were "entirely the result of her own indomitable energy."

At twenty-five, Bancroft was hired as the Director of Physical Culture for Brooklyn's public schools, allowing her to further spread the gospel of physical fitness for boys *and* girls in an age when strenuous activity was generally considered unladylike and even deleterious to a woman's metabolism. She also founded the American Posture League, a group that advocated on behalf of factory workers for more ergonomically correct workplaces. Bancroft strenuously argued that corsets and high heels were most unhealthful for a woman's posture, and she was even able to get the seats of New

York's subway cars altered to provide a better fit for riders.

For *Games for the Playground, Home, School and Gymnasium*, Bancroft proved to be ahead of her time yet again. Bancroft applied her energies to researching recreation among the varied immigrant populations of New York City. Her book was intended as a resource for teachers, and what a resource it was. *Games* was a celebration of international recreation dating from a time when ethnic diversity was, at best, tolerated.

Times have changed in the intervening century, but modern concerns over childhood obesity reveal how forward-thinking Jessie Bancroft was. Reading her work, I was struck with Bancroft's ability to imbue her games with a moral purpose while also making them sound enjoyable. She believed that games and exercise sharpened young minds and reduced sloth. For her, a good physical education was one of the most desirable goals to which our nation's schools could aspire. Of course, she was right. So while Jessie H. Bancroft was not legally able to vote for most of her lifetime, she found her own way of making a difference in the world.

In short, she *was* a remarkable woman, and it is an honor to present here some of the games from her book along with a goodly number of games from other sources and times.

But beware: Once you start playing the games in the following pages, *your* face is going to hurt—in a good way!

A NOTE ON TAGGING: Many of the games that follow involve chasing and tagging. Tagging must be done with an open hand on an appropriate part of the body anywhere from the neck down. (For questions about what constitutes "appropriate" sites, consult *The Pocket Guide to Mischief*.) "Clothing doesn't count," so something more substantial than another player's T-shirt must be touched.

ADULTS: Grownups don't need to be needlessly overseeing every aspect of children's play, but obviously, the larger the group, the more appropriate that an adult be on hand. Further, the adults do not simply have to mediate and officiate. Most of these games benefit from *more* players taking part in them, not fewer.

So divest yourself, Dear Reader, of that misguided sense of dignity and have some fun! But be sure to warm up and stretch out first, though. You don't want to be clutching your xiphoid in agony and crying out, *"Daddy isn't as spry as he used to be, kids. Now tell Mommy to call 911!"*

DIVIDING TEAMS: Having an adult present is also helpful when it comes time to make teams. While it is possible to have kids pick their own team members, the process is open to cries of injustice and favoritism. The resulting bad vibes and lawsuits tend to poison the game itself.

As an adult, you have a built-in persona of disinterested third party. So if you already have a fair-minded roster made up of who is on what team (and if you keep the ball rolling), most kids will make only token complaints before joining in the fun.

If you'd like to include the players in the process, ask the kids to pair off with someone of their choosing. They will then do so with their closest companion. Have these pairs stand facing each other. Players on the left are on Team A, and players on the right are on Team B. The best friends are now forced to play with other kids, widening their social network and making you feel quite clever.

With really large groups, have all of the players line up according to height. Then number consecutively in pairs (the two shortest kids being Pair One, and so on). These pairs then divide, one half going to one team and the other half to the opposite team.

Finally, purchasing various multi-sided dice is useful for times when one player is needed to be It. If you have eight players, you simply assign each player a number, one through eight. You then roll an eight-sided die, and It is painlessly selected.

A quick game of Humminna Humminna (see page 70) can also work to divide the group, as long as the Humminnator agrees to shout a number that's exactly half of the total group.

A BRIEF MEDITATION ON "IT": Since ancient times, innumerable game instructions have begun with "*A player is chosen to be It.*" But in our modern age, It has become the victim of tiresomely well-intentioned papers relating the psychological traumas of children who were designated as It in children's games.

This seems entirely wrong-headed. If a game is being played in the proper spirit, there is a certain glee in being It. In fact, adult observers must often have to make sure that no attention-hungry child is willfully being It time and again.[3] Being It should be considered a prized honor, and anyone who has worked with kids is familiar with the calls of "I want to be It!" "No, it's *my* turn to be It! You were It last time!"

LAST THING: While many of these games have lasted for centuries, they were all invented at some point. Their rules are not set in stone; feel free to alter them to suit your needs! If you have any notes or suggestions on games that you'd like to share, please e-mail them to me at kingbart@comcast.net.

PR means the game is Potentially Rough, and adults should monitor the activity to keep it within the bounds of appropriateness.

---

3. *Being It can also lead to amusing instructions. One of Ms. Bancroft's games originally read that the players must "clasp hands with It," which hardly sounds inviting.*

Active Games

If you're in charge of teaching and/or leading a game, your role is crucial: you are the leader, coach and referee. In addition, you are the host/hostess, group psychologist, and possibly a competitor. Now make us proud, and go have fun!

TIP: Many of the games in this chapter (and the book in general) involve teams competing to finish a contest or relay race. Try having everyone on a given team sit down once the team is done. That makes it easier to see what team finished first.

19

All Up Relay

★ *6-PLUS PLAYERS*
★ *PLAYGROUND, GYMNASIUM, SCHOOLROOM*

The players are divided into two or more groups. The groups line up in single file behind a starting line. Directly in front of each team, at the opposite end of the running space (which should be from 20 to 50 feet long), two circles are marked, each about 3 feet in diameter, and placed side by side, with rims touching. In one of the circles of each pair are three objects. Plastic pins or cones are good, but things such as unabridged dictionaries or narcoleptic rodents can also be used.

On a signal, Player Number One of each file runs forward and quickly moves the items from one circle to the other. If pins or cones are being used, they must be made to stand. No items can touch the outline of the circle. As Player Number One finishes, she runs back to her line, touches the next player on the hand, and then goes to the back of the line. The second player should be waiting for this "touch off" with toe on the starting line and hand outstretched.

On receiving the touch off, Player Number Two runs forward to the circles and changes the objects from the second ring back to the first, observing the same rules. Each player, in turn, does this. The group whose last player is first to dash over the starting line on his return wins the game.

If needed, or to make the game more challenging, referees can assess one foul against a team for 1) a runner starting over the line without the "touch off";

2) vertical items that are left horizontal; 3) items left standing outside the correct circle. The teams win in the order of finishing *plus* the lowest score on fouls. Thus, if team A finishes first with six fouls, team B finishes second with four fouls, and team C finishes third with no fouls, team C wins, being given first place, team B second place, and team A third place. Got it?

Animal Blind Man's Bluff

★ *6-PLUS PLAYERS*
★ *INDOORS, GYMNASIUM, PLAYGROUND*

One player is blindfolded and stands in the center of the group with a yardstick or baseball bat. At a safe distance, the other players walk or dance around him in a circle until he taps three times on the floor with his stick, when they must stand still. The blindfolded player then points his stick out. The closest player must silently step forward and take the opposite end of the stick in his hand.

The blindfolded player then commands him to make a noise like some animal, such as a dog, marmot, lion, donkey, duck, parrot, etc. From this the blind man tries to guess the name of the player. If the guess is correct, they change places. If wrong, the game is repeated.

The guesser can challenge the players by naming uncommon animals. The players should try to disguise their natural tones as much as possible when imitating the animals, and have fun trying to fool the guesser. Players may also disguise their height, to deceive the blind man, by bending their knees to seem shorter or rising on toes to seem taller.

With large groups, two players can be blindfolded.

Bacon!

★ *7-PLUS PLAYERS*
★ *PLAYGROUND, GYMNASIUM*

Two parallel lines are drawn on the ground anywhere from 30 to 50 feet apart. All of the players except one (who will be It) stand beyond one of these lines. In the middle territory between the lines is where It takes his place.

At some point, Player It will cry "Ham, ham, chicken, ham, BACON!" At the word "bacon," the other players must all rush across to the opposite line, being chased by the center player, who tags any that he can. Any player who is tagged joins him from then on in chasing the others.

The trick is that the center player, instead of saying "Ham, ham, chicken, ham, BACON," may trick or tantalize the runners by crying out "Ham, ham, chicken, ham, BOOGER," or "Ham, ham, chicken, ham, BILATERAL SYMMETRY," or anything else that he chooses. Any player who starts to run upon such a false alarm is considered a captive and must also join any players in the center.

Another way of giving a false alarm is for any one of the center players except the original It to say, "Ham, ham, chicken, ham, BACON!" Any runner starting in response to such a false signal also becomes captive and must join the players in the center.

The game ends when everyone is caught. The first player who was caught is the new center player, or It, for the next game.

Bear in the Pit PR

★ *7-PLUS PLAYERS*
★ *PLAYGROUND, GYMNASIUM*

A bear pit is formed by the players joining hands in a circle with one in the center as the bear. The bear tries to get out of

the circle by breaking apart his bars (the clasped hands), or by going over or under these barriers. Should the bear escape, all of the other players give chase, the one catching him becoming the new bear.

This is a favorite game with boys, and is not as rough as Bull in the Ring (page 30), for instance, because the bear can escape in a variety of ways. He can try to fool the other players by appearing to break through the bars in one place, and suddenly turning and crawling under another, and so forth. In the spirit of good play, the person who is the bear is discouraged from either biting or hibernating.

Blind Bell

★ *5-PLUS PLAYERS*
★ *INDOORS, GYMNASIUM, PLAYGROUND*

All the players but one are blindfolded and scatter about. The one who is *not* blindfolded carries a bell (or other sound-making device) loosely in one hand, so that it will ring with every step. If desired, this bell may be hung around the neck. The blindfolded players try to tag (touch) the one with the bell, who will have to be on the lookout to keep out of

27

their way. Whoever catches the bellman changes places with him.

Blindfolded players are encouraged not to run pell-mell, so as to avoid disaster.

Where there are more than twenty players, there can be two or more bellmen.

Body Guard

★ *6-PLUS PLAYERS*
★ *PLAYGROUND, GYMNASIUM*

Two small spaces are marked off at each end of the play area as a "home ground." One player is chosen to be the Mighty Panjandrum. This is an important person who requires two bodyguards. Thus, two other players are chosen to be these guards.

The game starts with these three players in one of the home grounds and the rest of the players outside of it. The Mighty Panjandrum and his bodyguards come forth, traveling from one home to the other, with the two bodyguards clasping each other by the hand and protecting the Panjandrum as a human shield. The object of the game is for the players at large to tag the Mighty Panjandrum without being tagged back by his guards. If a player successfully tags the Mighty Panjandrum, the group must go back to where they started and try again to reach the other home ground.

The guards will shift around their lord to block attacks from the group at large, and the Mighty Panjandrum himself may evade them by moving around inside of his guards' protection.

Whenever a guard succeeds in tagging another player, the Mighty Panjandrum and his guards return at once to the home; whereupon the player tagged changes places with the Mighty Panjandrum, and the game goes on as before.

If the Mighty Panjandrum can make it

safely across the playing area, he has won, and one of his loyal guards may change places with him for another attempt back.

Bull in the Ring PR

★ *7-PLUS PLAYERS*
★ *WRESTLING MAT OR GRASSY AREA*
★ *THIS IS A VERY ROUGH GAME*

All but one of the players stand in a circle with hands firmly clasped. The player who is It stands in the center and is the bull.

The idea of this game is simplicity itself: The bull tries to break through the ring by parting the hands of any two players. *No fair going under!* To prevent bull-fighting, review the safety rules carefully beforehand. For example, the bull isn't allowed to simply charge the ring players, and goring is also frowned upon.

If the bull breaks through the ring, the two

may come to his rescue and try to resist his being pulled over the line, either by pulling him in the opposite direction or by trying to secure a hold on one of the opponents. A player does not belong to the enemy until his entire body has been pulled over the line. He must then join his captors in trying to secure players from across the line. The group wins that has the largest number of players at the end of a time limit.

Catch of Fish

★ *8-PLUS PLAYERS*
★ *PLAYGROUND, GYMNASIUM*

A line is drawn across each end of the playground, beyond which the players stand in two equal parties, one at one end and one at the other. The players of one party clasp hands to form a fish net. The players in the other party are fish. At a given signal both advance toward the center of the playground, which represents a stream, the object of the

fish being to swim across to the opposite shore without being caught in the net. To do this they will naturally dodge around the ends of the net.

The net should enclose or encircle any fish that it catches. The fish caught SHOULD NOT try to break apart the clasped hands forming the net, but may escape only through the opening where the two ends come together. Should the net break at any point by the hands becoming unclasped, the fish are ALL allowed to escape, and the players go back to their respective goals and begin again.

Any fish caught in the net are part of the catch. They are not to be filleted, but they are out of the game until all the members of one side or another are caught.

After the net has made one catch, the sides exchange roles, those of the fish that are left forming the new net, and the first net crossing to the other side and becoming fish. The two sides continue exchanging places and parts until everyone on one side is caught, or until the end of a predetermined time limit.

For a really large number of players it is better to have two small nets instead of one large one, the dodging being livelier and the progress of the game more rapid in every way.

Catch the Cane

★ *4-PLUS PLAYERS*
★ *PLAYGROUND, GYMNASIUM, SCHOOLROOM*

This is an admirable game for making

35

alert and active any children whose senses have been dulled by electronic devices.

The players number off and stand in a circle or semicircle. One player stands in the center, with her finger on the top of an upright baseball bat, yardstick, or wand. Suddenly, she lifts her finger from the bat, at the same time calling the number assigned to one of the players. The person whose number is called must run forward and catch the bat before it falls to the floor. If that player fails, he must return to his place in the circle; if successful, he changes places with the center player.

The action is best if the one calling the numbers gives them in unexpected order, sometimes repeating a number that has recently been given (1,1,1), then giving a few in consecutive order (4,5,6), and then skipping over a long series (8,2,3), etc.

Centipede Tag

★ *9-PLUS PLAYERS (THE MORE, THE BETTER)*
★ *ANY LEVEL PLAYING AREA OUTDOORS*

There are many different running, chasing, and tagging games, but this one is unique because the chasing and tagging is done in groups.

To play Centipede Tag, you want to divide the players into groups of three or more. (It's okay if the groups are not exactly equal.) Line up the kids in each group, one after another. If you have hats available, have the player in the front of each line wear a hat. He is the head of the

37

centipede. (Even better, have him wear an antennae headband if you have some.)

The last kid in the row wears a flag football belt. Turn it so that one of the Velcro patches is on his back, and stick a flag there. No worries if you don't have this; a tube sock stuck in the waistband or fastened with a wooden clothespin will work just as well.

Once the centipedes have been outfitted, have the kids hold the waist of the child in front of them. Now you're ready to begin! Give a signal, and let the centipedes try to tag each other. To get a successful tag, the "head" of one centipede must pull the flag off another centipede's end. But while attempting to tag another centipede, the group must worry about being tagged themselves. This results in all sorts of delightful myriapodous antics!

Once one centipede is declared the winner, be sure to mix up the groups so the heads and tails join the middle of a new centipede.

Chickadeedee

★ *5 TO 10 PLAYERS*
★ *ANY SPACIOUS ROOM OR OUTDOORS*

If possible, this game should be played in a room where all light is shut out, so that the sense of hearing will be the only guide in the game. Failing that, the player who is It can be blindfolded.

It is seated on the floor in the center of the room, and holds a pillow. The object of the game is for this player to tag or touch

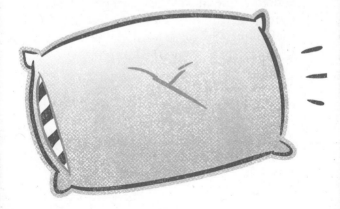

any of the other players with the pillow without leaving his sitting position on the floor. The object of the other players is to secretly approach as near as possible to It and then make a taunting cry of "Chicka-deedee!" close to his ear.

The game starts in perfect silence and darkness. A player steals up to the center man, calls "Chickadeedee!" and darts back again as quickly as possible, while It whirls his pillow around, trying to hit this player. While he is doing this, another player from some other direction may repeat the call of "Chickadeedee!" close to his ear, and darts back or dodges. Any tactics may be used for dodging, such as dropping to the floor or jumping.

Any player hit with the pillow exchanges places with the one in the center.

Chinese Wall

★ *8-PLUS PLAYERS*
★ *PLAYGROUND, LARGE BACKYARD, GYMNASIUM*

This is a fun game for both children and older players, as it involves some brisk running and dodging, especially if the play area is wide.

The Chinese Wall is marked off by two parallel lines 10 feet apart that run straight across the center of the play area. The space between the lines represents the Chinese Wall. On each side of the wall, at a distance of from 15 to 30 feet, a safety point or home goal is marked for the besiegers.

One player is chosen to defend the Chinese Wall, and takes his place upon it. All of the other players stand in one of the home goals. The defender calls "Attack if you dare!" At this point, all of the players must try to cross the wall to the home goal beyond. As the group crosses the

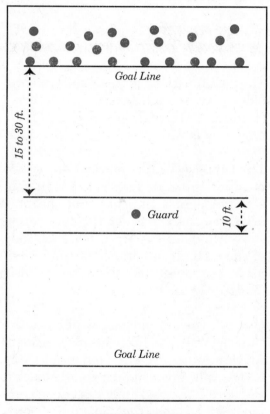

Goal Line

15 to 30 ft.

Guard

10 ft.

Goal Line

CHINESE WALL

wall, the defender tries to tag as many as he can, but he may not overstep the boundaries of the wall himself.

Anyone who is tagged joins the defender in trying to catch the rest of the players during future attacks.

Players continue to go back and forth from home goal to home goal. The game ends when all have been caught, the last player taken being defender for the next game.

Cross Tag

★ *5-PLUS PLAYERS*
★ *PLAYGROUND, GYMNASIUM*

One player is chosen to be It. She calls out the name of another player and starts chasing him. At any point in the chase, a third player may run *between* the one who is It and the one whom she is chasing. At that point, the third player becomes the new object of the chase.

You see where this is going? A fourth player may also then run between the chaser and her new "chasee," diverting the chase yet again. Of course, whenever It can tag a player, that player becomes the new It.

More fun can be made by the free players getting in the way of It without crossing between her and the player she is chasing.

For another fun version of tag, see *Japanese Tag* on page 73.

Don't Walk This Way

★ *6-PLUS PLAYERS*
★ *ANYWHERE*

This game is simple and hilarious. First, line up everyone side by side and set up a finishing line about 10 to 15 yards away from them. Then select a member of the group randomly ("Who has the closest birthday from right now?") and have that player go first.

For this person, the game will be easy. He or she simply crosses over to the finishing line. But let's assume that he or she walks. That means that once the first person crosses the goal line, whoever was standing to his or her left must now cross the goal line doing something *different* from the first person. In our example, that means that walking is now out.

So what's left? Kids can be ingenious, and they are also limber. Cartwheeling, running, crawling, walking backwards or sideways, crawling, twirling, skipping, etc., are all possibilities.

NOTE: If adults are in the group and are among the last to attempt a creative mode of locomotion, have paramedics nearby.

Duck on a Rock

★ *4 TO 30-PLUS PLAYERS*
★ *PLAYGROUND, GYMNASIUM*

Each player is provided with a ball or

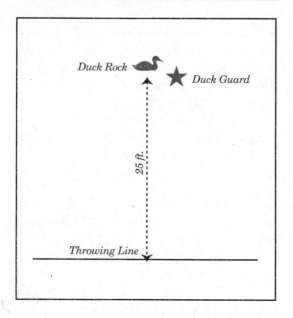

Duck Rock

Duck Guard

25 ft.

Throwing Line

DUCK ON A ROCK

rock, called a "duck." Anything about the size of a baseball or softball will work. A large rock, post, or even a stool is chosen as the *duck rock*, and 25 feet from it, a throwing line is drawn. (The game can also be played with bean bags, in which case one bag may be balanced on top of a

2-liter bottle weighted with a little water or sand in the bottom.)

A Guard is now selected by having all of the players throw their ducks at the duck rock from the throwing line. The one whose duck falls nearest to the rock becomes the first Guard.

The Guard approaches the duck rock and places his duck on it, then backs safely away at least 25 feet from the duck rock. The other players stand behind the throwing line and take turns in throwing at the guard's duck on the rock with their own ducks, trying to knock it from the rock.

After each throw, a player must recover his own duck and run back home beyond the throwing line. But first he must avoid the Guard. Should the player be tagged by the Guard while trying to get his duck, he must change places with the Guard. For his part, the Guard may tag a player at any time after he crosses the throwing line. If the player can make it to his duck, he can stand with his foot on it where the duck first fell and be considered "safe." But the player must eventually get back to the throwing line.

FINE POINTS: The Guard may not tag any player unless his own duck is still on the rock. So before he may chase the thrower, he must pick up his own duck and replace it first if it was knocked off. This replacing gives the thrower an opportunity to recover his own duck and run home; but if the Guard's duck was *not* displaced from the duck rock, the thrower may have to wait either on the other side of the throwing line or with his foot on his own duck if he can get to it.

When another thrower gets the attention of the Guard, any stranded runner may try to make it to his duck or back to the throwing line. Thus, several players may be waiting at once, some of them near the duck rock with a foot on their ducks waiting to return to the throwing line, others behind the throwing line waiting to get to their ducks.

Players may stand this way as long as necessary, awaiting an opportunity to run home; but the moment a player lifts his duck from the ground, or takes his foot from it, he may be tagged by the Guard. Having once lifted his duck to run home with it, a player may not again place it on the ground during that turn.

Again, any player tagged by the Guard must change places with him, placing his own duck on the rock. The old Guard must quickly recover his duck and run for the throwing line after tagging a player, as he in turn may be tagged as soon as the new Guard has placed his duck on the rock.

VARIATION: This game can be played by stacking multiple stones instead of having just one "duck" on top. The entire pile is then knocked over, and the Guard has to restack the stones before he can tag the other players. This version can be played on a flat beach, park, or playground.

El Globo

★ *2-PLUS PLAYERS*
★ *OUTSIDE*
★ *WATER BALLOON, WIFFLE BAT, TREE OR POLE*

If you know how to play *Piñata*, you know how to play *El Globo*. It's usually played in warm weather by people who don't mind getting wet. To start, fill several balloons with water, and hang one from a tree. Or put up more than one balloon to improve the odds.

Then blindfold one of the players, spin her around, and hand her the bat. Position the slightly dizzy player within reach of the balloon! (It's better if the bat is plastic in case she loses her grip.) When the batter hits the balloon, everyone should shout "El Globo!"

It is possible to play El Globo when the

blindfolded person *thinks* he or she is swinging at a piñata. Show the player the piñata, and then after the blindfolding, switch the piñata with a water balloon.

End Ball

★ *12-PLUS PLAYERS AND A REFEREE*
★ *PLAYGROUND, GYMNASIUM*

A volleyball or basketball can work for this game. For a playing space, any area measuring about 30 x 30 feet works. (Half of a basketball court is 46 x 50 feet; this size also works fine.) The field should be divided across the center by a straight line from side to side. Finally, at either end of the playing area, a narrow goal strip about 3 feet wide should be marked with a line parallel to the end line.

The players are divided into two teams. One third of the players of each team take their places within the goal at one end of the ground. They are called the Basemen. All other team members scatter in the open area in front of the goal on the *opposite* side of the field. These are the Guards.

The object of the game is for the Guards on one side to throw the ball *over* the heads of the opposing Guards on the opposite side to their own Basemen. The ball can also be bounced or rolled, though these passes are easier to intercept.

Each ball caught by a Baseman scores one point for that team. *After a goal is made, the ball remains in play.* The Baseman then throws the ball back over the heads of the opposing Guards to his own team's Guards for another try.

Competing Guards try to intercept the ball before it can reach the Basemen behind them. If successful, they then throw the ball to their own Basemen on the other side of the field.

If the ball goes out of bounds, the last team to touch it loses possession. The referee should give the ball to the opposing team player closest to where the ball went out of bounds.

The referee starts the game by tossing the ball upward between two opposing

Guards and letting them grab or tip it. Play can go off of a running clock, or until a certain point limit is reached.

FOULS

Fouls are given for any player stepping on or over his or her assigned territory with one foot or both, either over the side lines or into the opponent's court. No ball caught on a foul scores.

It is a foul for Guards to carry the ball for more than one step. (This encourages quick passing and keeps players moving around to get open.) Basemen with the ball can slide along as much as they like.

It is a foul to touch the ball while it is in the hands of another player. A pass can be blocked only *after* a player throws it.

It is a foul to hold or push another player.

Fouls are "punished" by giving the ball to the nearest guard of the opposing team, who can immediately put it in play with a throw to a teammate.

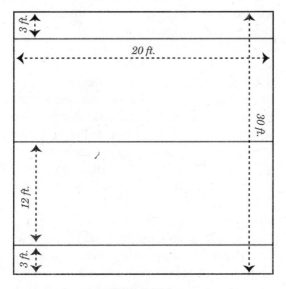

END BALL

Exchange

★ *5 TO 30 PLAYERS*
★ *INDOORS, GYMNASIUM, PLAYGROUND*

Enough chairs for all the players minus one are set up in a circle, facing the middle. One player is blindfolded and stands in the center. The other players sit in chairs arranged around him, and the players are numbered consecutively from one to the highest number playing.

The players can sit in consecutive order, or they may change places at the outset to confuse the blindfolded player. The blindfolded player then calls out any two of the assigned numbers, whereupon the players bearing those numbers must exchange places. While they do this, the blindfolded player will try to tag one of the players OR to secure one of the temporarily empty chairs. Any player tagged or having his chair taken must yield his chair to the blindfolded player. No player may go outside of the circle of chairs, but any other tactics may be resorted to for evading capture, such as stooping, creeping, dashing, or contortionism.

Forcing the City Gates PR

★ *10 TO 30 OR MORE PLAYERS*
★ *PLAYGROUND, GYMNASIUM*

The players are divided into two teams. The two sides then line up in two straight lines, facing each other about 10 feet apart or less. Each of these lines represents the gates of a city. The players hold hands. (It's best to alternate larger or stronger players with the smaller ones.)

Each team has a player who is its General. The General of one side names one of his players, who steps forward and tries to break *through* or dodge *under* (not over) the hands of the opposing side. If he does not succeed in one place, he may try in another, but may not have more than three trials lasting five seconds each.

Should this player *succeed* in breaking or dodging under the opposing line, he returns to his side, taking the two opposing players whose hands were broken apart or evaded. These prisoners now reinforce his side. The players taken from the opposing side must work for the side to which they are taken captive, each prisoner being placed in the line between two of the original team.

Should the player fail in his third attempt, he is to remain on the side of his opponents and help them.

The Generals alternate turns in sending forth a man to "force the city gates." The side wins that eventually secures all of the opposing players OR that has more players at the end of a predetermined time. The action may be made more rapid where a large number are playing by sending out two or more players at once.

NOTE: Adults should encourage sportsmanship and disallow inappropriate strategies (e.g., rope burns) on the part of players forcing the gates.

Fox Trail

★ *3 TO 20 PLAYERS*
★ *OUTDOORS, SNOW, SEASHORE, GYMNASIUM*

This is a simple snow game, but may be played anywhere that a large diagram may be outlined on the ground.

Mark a large circle from 20 to 30 feet in diameter on the ground and cross it with intersecting lines like the spokes of a wheel, there being about 4 such lines (making a total of 8 spokes). The more players there are, the larger the circle and the greater the number of spokes; but there is no fixed relation between the number of spokes and players.

One player is chosen to be the Hunter. The Hunter stands in the center, that is, on the hub of the wheel. The other players scatter around the rim and are Foxes. They are not stationed at any one point, but run or

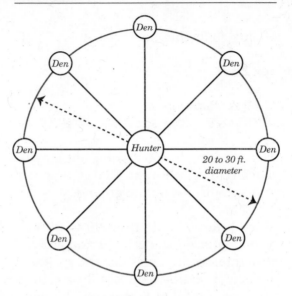

FOX TRAIL

stand anywhere around the rim when not dashing across the spokes.

The object of the game is for the Foxes to cross the wheel to some opposite point without being tagged by the Hunter. They may only run, however, on the trails—that is, on the lines of the diagram. Once they get to the hub, they may turn on an angle at the hub and seek refuge on another spoke if necessary.

The Hunter changes places with anyone whom he tags.

Good Morning

★ *5-PLUS PLAYERS*
★ *INDOORS*

This game is best for younger children. A child is chosen to be the Guesser. This player will be blindfolded, or at the very least, turn her back to the group. The leader then silently points to some other player in the group, who rises at once and says, "Good morning, Mariam!" (or whatever the child's name may be). The little Guesser, if she has recognized the voice, responds with, "Good morning, Arthur!" (or whomever else she thinks it is).

Depending on the group's size, if the Guesser does not guess the voice after the first greeting, the child may be required to repeat it, until the Guesser has had up to three attempts. Should she fail on the third trial, the Guesser turns around to see who the player was, and changes places with him. If she names the right player, the Guesser retains her position until she fails to guess the voice of the one greeting her.

Other players should be required to change their seats after the Guesser has blinded her eyes, so that she will not be assisted in her judgment by remembering where players were sitting.

For a twist, a person from another room, neighborhood, or country may be called in. Should a strange voice be heard in this way, the little Guesser is considered correct if she answers, "Good morning, stranger!"

Good vs. Evil

★ *8-PLUS PLAYERS AND A REFEREE*
★ *ANY OPEN SPACE*

For this epic battle, two parallel lines are

marked about 10 feet apart across the center of a play area. The space between these two lines is the DMZ (a neutral area called the Demilitarized Zone).

At a distance beyond each line, and parallel to it, a second line is marked.

GOOD vs. EVIL

The space beyond this line is a Refuge for players of the party belonging to that side. This second line should be at a good distance from the DMZ, so as to give space for a good chase during the game.

The players are divided into two teams, Good and Evil, which each line up toeing the line on either side of the DMZ. The parties choose a representative to meet inside the DMZ.

A die or coin is used to figure out who will retreat first. The representatives agree that a die roll of 1 to 3 is Good and 4 to 6 is Evil. (With a coin, heads can be Good, tails Evil.) One of the reps then rolls the die or tosses the coin.

If Good's side comes up, the Good team must turn and run for the goal behind them, with the Evil team chasing them! Any Good player who is tagged has to freeze. The Evil team must *carry* this prisoner back to their home goal. Teams score one point for each prisoner caught,

players whose hands he parted give chase, with the one catching him becoming the next bull. If neither can catch him, play is stopped because of "no bull." Another bull must then be selected.

31

Catch and Pull Tug of War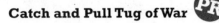

★ *8-PLUS PLAYERS*
★ *GYMNASIUM, PLAYGROUND*

Any number of players may engage in this contest, which is one of the best games for a large number of kids.

A line is drawn down the middle of the playing space. The players are divided into two groups, with the groups standing on opposite sides of the line. The players must stay close to the line, and cannot cross over it to the other side.

The game starts on a signal and consists in catching hold of an opponent by any part of his body—a hand, arm, or foot—reaching over the line and so pulling him across the boundary. This will result in much hullaballoo and many cries of "Jiminy! They've got ahold of me foot!"

Any number of players may try to secure a hold on an opponent and any number but the prisoner must be carried (no dragging!) all the way back to the goal. Prisoners cannot resist, but they may go limp.[1] The party first scoring a certain number of points wins, or there can be a time limit with high score winning.

One rule that can be observed is to have the tagger carry his prisoner piggyback to his goal. To do this, have the players line up according to size at the opening of the game, so that the tall and small players are placed opposite each other.

Hide the Thimble

★ *5 TO 60 PLAYERS*
★ *INDOORS*

YOUNGER PLAYERS VERSION:

One player is shown a thimble, cork, ring, or other small object, and is then sent from the room. In the player's absence,

---

1. *Any carried prisoner who is accidentally or unceremoniously dropped is considered free to return to his team.*

the object is hidden in the room. When
the object is hidden, the absent player
is recalled, and proceeds to hunt for the
hidden object. While he is doing this, the
others sing or clap their hands, the sound
being very soft and low when the hunter
is far away from the object, and growing
louder as he approaches it.

PROFICIENT PLAYERS VERSION:

Again, a thimble, cork, ring, or other small object may be used for hiding. All of the players leave the room except one, who places the object in plain sight but where it would not be likely to be seen. It may be placed behind any other object, as long as it can be seen there without moving any object. This hiding will be especially successful if some hiding place can be found near the color of the object, for instance, if the object were transparent, it could be taped to the window. If it were metal, it could be hanging from the door handle.

When the object has been placed, the players are called into the room, and all begin to look for it. When a player spies the object, he quietly takes his seat. Once seated, the player can say, *"Huckle, buckle, bean stalk!"* (or some other memorable phrase) which indicates that he knows where the object is. The game keeps on until all of the players have located the object, or until the leader calls the hunt closed.

Of course, some of those seated might be "faking" it so as not to be the last one, so the leader calls upon someone to identify the item's location. The first one who found the object should hide it for the next game.

Hot Lava Monster

★ *4-PLUS PLAYERS*
★ *PLAY STRUCTURE ON PLAYGROUND*

Scientists believe that the Hot Lava Monster (HLM) was originally the lost child of a geologist and a troll. Whatever its origins, the HLM's game is particularly enjoyed by younger children, who enjoy its simple elegance.

One player is chosen to be the Hot Lava Monster. This fearsome creature has one flaw: he must always keep one foot on the ground at ALL times. That means that the HLM cannot climb (very far) up a play structure. But he can run beneath it, reaching upwards!

The other players clamber up the play structure, and then the HLM is released. The dreaded beast can bellow and bluster as he pursues his innocent victims and tries to tag them from below. For their part, the other children do their best to escape the HLM's clutches. Once a player is tagged, a new HLM is born. The old HLM climbs up the playground structure, and play begins anew.

To ensure that game play continues until the children get tired of it (or the parents do), make a rule that the kids on the play structure must attempt to migrate from one portion of it to another, and further, that the HLM cannot simply lie in wait at a strategic spot (like a bridge) but must also remain in motion.

Humminna Humminna

★ AN EVEN-NUMBERED GROUP
★ ANYWHERE

This very silly game is beloved by large groups of small children. It's very simple. The children are loosely scattered while an adult or kid who's good at math wanders among them saying, *"Humminna, humminna, humminna...."*

At some point this person will interrupt the "Humminnas" by shouting a number, e.g., *"Four!"* The children then try to sit down together in a group of four as quickly as possible. As shouting "Seven!" to a group of ten may lead to a riot, the Humminnator must be astute enough to shout only a number that will factor into the group's overall number.

Elimination is not necessary with this game, though it can be done with participants with the wrong group size or who sit down last.

NOTE: Accomplished Humminnators will periodically shout "One!" or even "Zero!" to the amusement of all.

Japanese Crab Race

★ *2-PLUS PLAYERS*
★ *ANYWHERE*

Until you try this, it's impossible to realize how badly you'll lose your sense of direction.

If there are just a few players for this game, it may be played as a simple race, without the relay described below.

The players line up behind a starting line in single files, each containing the same number of players. Opposite each file, at a distance of 20 to 40 feet, is a goal of some kind. (It can be a cone, line, circle, etc.) The game consists in a backwards race run on "all fours."

To start, the first player in each file gets in position, with his heels on the starting line and his back to the goal for which he is to run. All start together at a signal. The player who first reaches his goal scores one point for his team. Others follow in turn.

Japanese Tag

★ *4-PLUS PLAYERS*
★ *ANYWHERE*

One player is It, and tries to touch or tag one of the other players. In this form of the game, however, the player who is tagged must place his left hand on the spot touched, whether it be his back, knee, elbow, ankle, or any other part of the body. In that position, the new It must chase the other players. He is relieved of this position only when he succeeds in tagging someone else. The one tagged then becomes the chaser and must place her left hand on the place she was tagged. Laughter ensues.

Jumping Rope

★ *3-PLUS PLAYERS FOR GROUP PLAY*
★ *GYMNASIUM OR OUTDOORS*

Jump rope historians believe that the practice dates back to the ancient

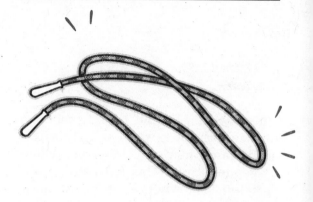

Egyptians, who are shown in artwork jumping over vines. (No, I'm not making this up.) Today, most people choosing a rope for singleton jumping get one that is about 6 feet long. A good rule of vine . . . er, thumb . . . is to have the rope just long enough to reach to the shoulders on each side while the player is standing on it.

Before trying the team feats below, the jumper should already be able to individually jump rope repeatedly on either foot, skip while jump-roping, and also be able to jump rope with the rope going backwards.

A long rope should be from 10 to 20 feet in length and should be turned by two players while one or more jumpers jump.

I. ONE LARGE ROPE

1. TWO TURNERS ARE TURNING THE ROPE SO THAT IT GOES TOWARD THE JUMPER. THE JUMPER SHOULD RUN UNDER IT AND BEGIN JUMPING. ONCE THIS IS DONE SUCCESSFULLY, THE JUMPER SHOULD TRY RUNNING IN, JUMPING ONCE, AND RUNNING OUT ON THE OPPOSITE SIDE. ANOTHER JUMPER SHOULD THEN FOLLOW.

2. WITH THE ROPE TURNING AWAY FROM THE JUMPER, THE JUMPER RUNS UNDER IT. AS ABOVE, THE NEXT STEP OF DIFFICULTY IS TO RUN IN, JUMP ONCE, AND RUN OUT ON THE OPPOSITE SIDE.

3. WITH THE ROPE GOING EITHER WAY, THE JUMPER RUNS IN, JUMPS ONCE, AND RUNS OUT BACKWARDS.

4. THE PLAYER RUNS IN AND JUMPS WHILE THE TURNERS SAY, "SALT, PEPPER, MUSTARD, CIDER,

VINEGAR," INCREASING THE ROPE'S TURNING SPEED
ON THE WORD "VINEGAR."

5. RUNNING AND SKIPPING, ONE JUMPER JUMPS IN
   WHILE REPEATING ANY VERSE OR SONG, E.G.:

"CINDERELLA

DRESSED IN YELLA

WENT UPSTAIRS TO KISS A FELLA

MADE A MISTAKE

AND KISSED A SNAKE

HOW MANY DOCTORS

DID IT TAKE?

1, 2, 3, ETC."

THE COUNTING CONTINUES UNTIL THE JUMPER
MISSES A JUMP.

6. SAME AS THE ABOVE WITH TWO JUMPERS FACING EACH OTHER, WITH THEIR INNER HANDS RESTING ON EACH OTHER'S SHOULDERS.

7. ONE OR TWO JUMPERS RUN IN AND JUMP FIVE TIMES WITH THEIR HANDS PLACED IN SOME PARTICULAR POSITION, SUCH AS HELD OUT SIDEWAYS AT SHOULDER LEVEL, CLASPED BEHIND, PLACED ON THE SHOULDERS, HEAD, OR HIPS, ETC.

8. ONE OR TWO JUMPERS RUN IN AND JUMP IN VARIOUS WAYS: BOTH FEET AT ONCE; ON ONE FOOT; ON THE OTHER FOOT; ON ALTERNATE FEET WITH A ROCKING STEP, CHANGING FROM ONE FOOT TO THE OTHER, ETC.

9. "CHASE THE FOX": THE JUMPERS CHOOSE A LEADER (THE FOX) WHO GOES THROUGH VARIOUS JUMPS, WITH THE OTHERS FOLLOWING IN SINGLE FILE AND COPYING.

10. "CALLING IN": A PLAYER RUNS IN AND JUMPS THREE TIMES, CALLING SOMEONE ELSE IN BY NAME ON THE SECOND JUMP. THEY JUMP ONCE TOGETHER, AND THE FIRST PLAYER RUNS OUT ON THE OPPOSITE SIDE. THE SECOND PLAYER, IN TURN, CALLS SOMEONE IN

ON HIS SECOND JUMP, ETC. PLAYERS WILL NEED TO
RUN OUT ON OPPOSITE SIDES.

11. "BEGGING": TWO PLAYERS RUN INTO THE ROPE AND
JUMP TOGETHER SIDE BY SIDE. WHILE JUMPING,
THEY CHANGE PLACES. ONE PLAYER STARTS THIS BY
SAYING, "GIVE ME SOME BREAD AND BUTTER," AND
THE OTHER, WHILE CHANGING, ANSWERS, "TRY MY
NEXT-DOOR NEIGHBOR." THIS IS CONTINUED UNTIL
ONE TRIPS.

12. "MAD SPRINGS": A PLAYER RUNS IN, TURNS HALFWAY
OR ALL THE WAY AROUND IN TWO JUMPS, AND RUNS
OUT ON THE SAME SIDE.

13. "WINDING THE CLOCK": A PLAYER RUNS IN, COUNTS
CONSECUTIVELY FROM ONE TO TWELVE, TURNING
HALFWAY AROUND EACH TIME, AND THEN RUNS
OUT.

II. TWO ROPES

Using two ropes at one time requires
considerable skill of both the turners
and jumpers. When two ropes are turned
inward toward each other, the turn is

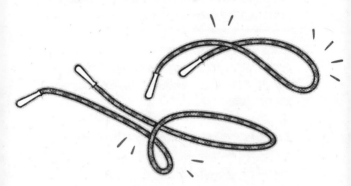

called "*Double Dutch*," or "*Double Dodge*."
When the two ropes are turned outward,
away from each other, the turn is called
"*French Rope*."

All the "fancy" jumps described earlier
can be done in either style.

Particularly interesting are jumps using
one large rope and one small rope. While
two turners keep the large rope turning,
a player turning and skipping her own
small rope can go through the following
feats:

1. THE PLAYER STANDS IN AND BOTH THE LARGE AND SMALL ROPES START TOGETHER.

2. WHILE TURNING AND SKIPPING HER OWN INDIVIDUAL ROPE, THE PLAYER RUNS UNDER THE LARGE ROPE. THE PLAYER THEN RUNS OUT EITHER BACKWARD OR FORWARD.

3. THE PLAYER RUNS IN WHILE TURNING HIS INDIVIDUAL ROPE BACKWARD WHILE THE BIG ROPE GOES FORWARD, OR VICE-VERSA.

4. A PLAYER JUMPS IN THE LARGE ROPE, AT THE SAME TIME TURNING AND JUMPING IN HER OWN INDIVIDUAL ROPE. ANOTHER PLAYER RUNS IN, FACING HER, IN THE SMALL ROPE, JUMPS WITH HER, AND THEN RUNS OUT AGAIN WITHOUT STOPPING EITHER ROPE.

Old-School I Spy

★ 3-PLUS PLAYERS
★ ANYWHERE

One player is chosen to be the Spy. The Spy blinds his eyes at a "safe house" while

the other players scatter and hide. The
Spy counts loudly aloud up to anywhere
from 35 to 100.

Upon completion, the Spy announces his
readiness to take up the hunt by shouting
aloud, "Coming!" or merely the last count
(e.g., "One hundred!") The Spy immediately tries to detect as many hidden
players as possible. For each player the
Spy spots, he dashes back to the safe
house and hits it three times while calling
out, "One, two, three," and then naming
the player.

The first one caught by the Spy this way
becomes the Spy for the next game.

However, as soon as a player knows he
has been detected by the Spy, he should
race to the safe house. Once there, he
should hit it three times and call out,
"One, two, three for me!"

What makes the game fun is that *any
player* who does this after the spy has

started on his hunt may save himself in this way, whether he has been detected or not. This keeps all the players on their toes.

Should the Spy make a mistake in identity, the player *really* seen and the one named by mistake are both free and may return to the safe house without further danger.

Partner Tag

★ *6-PLUS PLAYERS (BUT IT NEEDS TO BE AN EVEN NUMBER)*
★ *OUTDOORS, GYMNASIUM*

One player is chosen as It and another as the Runner. All of the other players pair off by hooking arms. These pairs then spread out a reasonable distance. (It is helpful to have some boundaries for the playing area so that the action doesn't spread too far.)

Play begins with the Runner trying to

save himself from being tagged. The Runner does this by hooking arms with either member of any pair he chooses. Whenever a Runner does this, the *third* party of that group becomes the new Runner and must save himself the same way. If the Runner is tagged at any time, he becomes It and the player formerly known as It becomes the new Runner.

To add fun, the couples should run and twist away from the Runner (but they must make their arms available), who is liable at any time to lock arms with one of them and so make the other a Runner.

Pebble Chase

★ *4-PLUS PLAYERS*
★ *ANY OPEN AREA*

One player (the Pebble Holder) clasps a small pebble between the palms of his hands. The other players stand grouped around him, each with his hands extended, thumbs on the outside and palms touching.

The Pebble Holder puts his hands between the palms of each player and seems to drop the pebble, concealing who it is going to.[2] That's because the player who actually *receives* the pebble will be chased by the others, and can only be saved by running back to the Pebble Holder and giving the pebble to him. (The Pebble Holder cannot run away and must accept the pebble back.)

This chase may begin as soon as the players suspect who has the pebble. Therefore, each player should carefully watch the hands and faces of the others to detect who gets it. Once a decision is made, the chase begins.

It is in the interest of the player who *gets* the pebble to conceal this fact until the

---

2. *As he makes his rounds, the Pebble Holder may choose to say things like, "Do not try to snatch the pebble from my hand, Grasshopper."*

attention of the group is distracted from him, when he may slip away and get a good headstart before he is detected. He may do this whenever he sees fit, but by the time the leader has passed the last pair of hands, he can wait no longer.

If the person being chased can get back to the Pebble Holder and gives him the pebble before being tagged, he continues with the group. If he is tagged, he must change places with the Pebble Holder.

Poison

★ *8-PLUS PLAYERS*
★ *ANY LARGE AREA*

A circular playing area is marked by having the players clasp hands, forming a circle, and then taking two steps in. A Home Base is then designated some distance from this playing area.

The game begins by having the players clasp hands around the outside of the

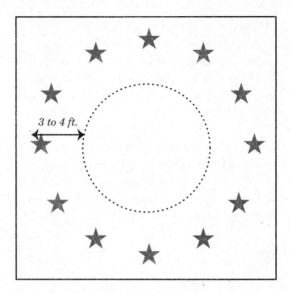

3 to 4 ft.

POISON

circle again. On a signal, each player tries, by pulling or twisting (no tripping!), to get others to step within the smaller circle, all the while staying out of it himself.

Anyone who touches the ground *on* or *within* the inner circle, even with one foot, is said to be poisoned. As soon as this happens, the player (or players) so poisoned become Catchers; the other players shout "Poisoned!" and at once break the circle and run for safety. The Catcher(s) try to tag those fleeing before they make it to the Home Base.

Anyone tagged before reaching Home Base joins the Catchers. For the next round, the Catchers stand inside the ring, ready to give chase. The game continues until there are not enough people to surround the circle, at which point all Catchers are released.

Popcorn Bowling

★ *2-PLUS PLAYERS*
★ *HARDWOOD OR LEVEL PAVED AREA OUTDOORS*
★ *EMPTY LITER JUGS, LOTS OF UNPOPPED POPCORN*

Although automated bowling alleys took the fun out of bowling at home, now it's time to reclaim our right to roll strikes in the driveway. First, take ten empty plastic liter jugs and fill them with unpopped popcorn. Yes, that's a lot of popcorn, but as long as the bottles are washed out, you can still pop the corn later. Number the bottles from 1 to 10 with a marking pen.

Popcorn is used because the pins make such a cool noise when they bang into each other and fall down. Of course, rocks, dirt, or puffed rice can be used as bottle filler instead.

Next, set up the pins on a level surface (about 9 inches apart in every direction) in the pattern you see below. Although a flat driveway is good, a well-mowed lawn can also work. Remember, you need to be able to roll your ball at them from a distance of at least 20 feet away. *Caution: balls are not to be rolled toward a road and children must never run into the road to chase a ball.*

Any round ball can be used for popcorn bowling. The beauty of the game is that these pins will make a lot of noise when they get hit by the ball and start bouncing off of each other!

To keep score, add up the numbers on the bottles that are knocked over with each roll.

Potato Race

★ *6-PLUS PLAYERS*
★ *INDOORS, PLAYGROUND, GYMNASIUM*

This potato race can also be played with eggs, though this is generally a waste of eggs.

The players are divided into groups that line up in single file. Placed on the floor in front of each group is a row of potatoes at intervals of 2 or 3 feet apart. There should be one potato for each player in the file. The larger and the more irregular in shape the potatoes the better.

Each leader is given a teaspoon, and beside the leader of the row is a pan, box, or basket, in which the potatoes are to be placed. At a signal each leader starts forward, takes up a potato on the spoon, carries it to his box and places the potato in it. The potato can *only* be touched by the spoon! When successful, the first player then hands the spoon to the next player in line.

Should a potato be touched with something besides the spoon, the player must replace it and pick it up again on the spoon. Should a potato drop from the spoon, it must be picked up on the spoon where it dropped, and the play continued from that point.

The second player picks up the next potato, puts it in the box, and so on, until all have played, the last one standing beside the box with the spoon held up, signaling that he has finished.

NOTE: Do not let small children engage in this event before meals, as tater tots may prove distracting to the contestants.

Prisoner's Base

★ *6-PLUS PLAYERS*
★ *ANY LARGE, OPEN AREA*

This game has proven to be both ageless

and popular. In fact, Prisoner's Base was *so* popular in the 1300s, it was prohibited by the British Parliament because

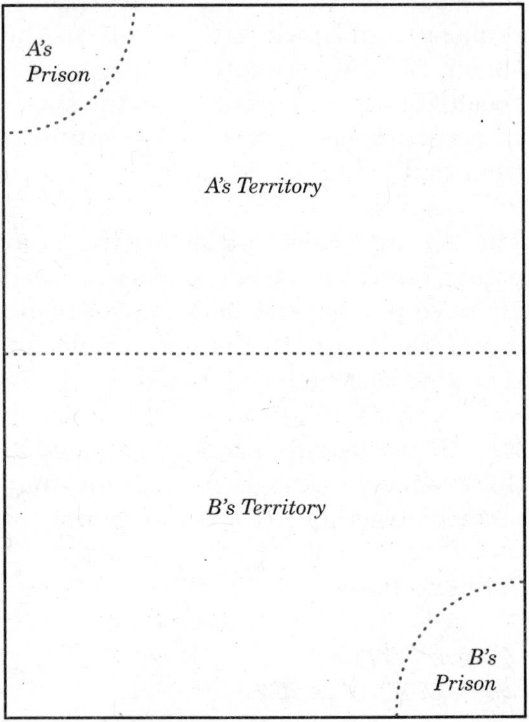

A's
Prison

A's Territory

B's Territory

B's
Prison

PRISONER'S BASE

the game caused too much of a commotion near Westminster. (At that time, the game was played by adults!) It is based on border warfare, and allows for judgment, prowess, and daring on the part of its players. There is also a role for G-rated trash talking. Enjoy.

VERSION 1

Mark off or use a playing area that is about 30 by 50 feet. The opposite corners of the field are the "prisons." (If you play in a street, the curb could be the boundary and the sidewalk could be where you put the prison.) With chalk or tape, mark a line across the middle of the playing area.

NOTE: Prisons and bases don't have to be exactly where the diagram shows. The key is to have the prison placed far enough away to make the freeing of prisoners challenging but possible.

Two equal armies are formed, and each

army goes to one half of the field. There are no prisoners at this time! A member from one army steps forward to the border and dares someone from the other army to meet him. Now the fun starts.

The key of this game is tagging. A player can only get tagged when he is on the *other* army's side. As always, only physical contact made on another player's body is a tag. (Clothing doesn't count.)

Players begin trying to sneak into the territory of their opponent. If they are tagged when even one foot is on enemy territory, they go to their enemy's prison, where they must stay until they are rescued or the game ends. (If ALL of them get put in prison, the game's over.) But why would a player try to sneak onto enemy territory?

1. *YOU WIN THE GAME IF YOU ENTER THE ENEMY'S PRISON WHEN IT'S EMPTY! (THAT IS, IT HOLDS NO PRISONERS.) THUS, IT'S A GOOD STRATEGY TO ENGAGE THE ENEMY ON ONE SIDE OF THE GROUND,*

WHILE A GOOD RUNNER IS HELD IN RESERVE TO DASH INTO THE ENEMY'S GOAL ON THE OTHER SIDE.

2. *IF SOMEONE FROM YOUR ARMY IS IN PRISON, YOU CAN SET HIM/HER FREE BY GETTING TO THE PRISON AND TAGGING HIM/HER. IF YOU CAN DO THIS, YOU ARE BOTH GUARANTEED SAFE PASSAGE BACK TO YOUR SIDE OF THE FIELD. OF COURSE, THE RESCUER MAY BE TAGGED BEFORE HE TOUCHES THE PRISONER, MAKING HIM A PRISONER TOO.*

3. *PLAYERS CAN TAUNT OPPONENTS BY GOING INTO THEIR TERRITORY AND LEAPING BACK BEFORE GETTING TAGGED. HOWEVER, ANY PLAYER WHO ACTUALLY GOES OUT OF BOUNDS GOES TO PRISON ALSO.*

Prisoner's Base comes complete with retreat and rally, charge and rout, and triumph (yay!) and despair (rats). If no player can make it to the enemy's empty prison to win the game outright, the game can also be played for a time limit. The team with the most prisoners at the end of the time then wins.

THE ULTIMATE PRISONER'S BASE

★ 6-PLUS PLAYERS AND A REFEREE

This advanced version of Prisoner's Base is not for the fainthearted. The ground is divided according to the diagram, and the players are divided into two equal armies. It is also necessary for each army to have a captain.

The captains are stationed at their respective bases, which are located at the *same* end of the grounds (instead of at opposite ends). The prison belonging to each side is located directly *opposite* its own home goal at the farther end of the ground, instead of near it.

One team goes first. A member of this side runs out to the middle of the ground and gives a taunt of some kind. ("*You smell like a bunch of hot buttered chimps!*") As soon as he has called this (but not before), he can be tagged by the opponents, who try to catch him before he can

run home again. Should he reach home
in safety, the opponents take their turn
in sending a man to the middle to give

ULTIMATE PRISONER'S BASE

a "dare" in the same way. A player need not run home, however, but may simply run away. Another player from his side can run out to protect him by trying to tag his opponents. Thus, several players from each team may be out in this way at one time.

A player may be caught by any man who left his home goal *after* he did, but by none who left *before* him. The referee and each player must therefore keep a sharp watch on his opponents to know which of them may tag him and which he may tag. With large groups, it's a good idea to restrict how many players can be out of the base at one time.

When a player is tagged, he is taken by his captor to prison. A captor may not be tagged while taking a prisoner to prison, and is allowed safe passage back to his base afterward. As with the original Prisoner's Base, if a player can reach the opponent's prison *without* being tagged by an opponent, he releases the first prisoner taken there and both players may return home without being tagged.

The object of the game is to imprison all of the other players, and when that is accomplished, to take possession of the opponent's home goal. Once this is done, the two parties change sides and begin again, the losing side being first to send a man into the field.

Robbers and Soldiers

★ *6-PLUS PLAYERS*
★ *BIG OUTDOORS AREA*

This Danish game is best played in a woodsy area, where there are many spots in which the robbers may hide. Old clothes are recommended.

The players are divided between Robbers and Soldiers, with about one Robber to every five Soldiers. (Faster players make better Robbers.)

The Soldiers have one General who directs their movements, and the Robbers (if there's more than one) have a Crime Lord. The Robbers are given five minutes headstart from a prison. The Soldiers wait at the prison until the General gives the command for the search to begin.

The object of the Robbers is to hide, and if found, to avoid capture if possible. They may hide by climbing trees or dodging behind them, concealing themselves in underbrush, beneath dead leaves, etc.

The Soldiers, in attempting to locate the Robbers, should use strategy. For instance, they could form a large circle and gradually work in toward the center, thus surrounding any Robbers who may be hidden within the territory so covered. As in ancient days, the Soldiers will find whistles or walkie-talkies of advantage for signaling each other for help.

For capture, the Robbers have to be tagged by *two* different Soldiers within a few seconds' time. The game is won when all of the Robbers have been made prisoners. If the Robbers can elude capture for a certain time limit (time being kept by the Crime Lord and/or General), they win.

Run for Your Lives!

★ *6-PLUS PLAYERS*
★ *OUTDOOR AREA WITH PLENTY OF BUSHES OR OTHER CAMOUFLAGE*

This Danish game is a form of Hide-and-Seek, but the hiding and the seeking are done by parties instead of individually. (Despite its histrionic name, the game is not life-threatening.[3])

Two teams are chosen, each with its own captain. One party becomes the Search Party and remains at the home base, while the Hiding Party goes out with its captain, who helps the various individuals

---

3. *You know how melodramatic the Danes can be.*

find good hiding places.

When all are hidden, the Hiding Party's captain goes back to the Search Party, who at once start out on the hunt. This party may divide up or not, as its captain sees fit, but *none* may remain behind or loiter near the home base.

The captain of the Hiding Party accompanies the Search Party, calling out signals to his hidden teammates. This lets them know where the Searchers are and allows them to sneak nearer to the home base by dodging from one hiding place to another.

Said captain may wish to shout out signals like the following examples:

"RED!" = DANGER

"GREEN!" = WE'RE NOT EVEN CLOSE

"PURPLE!" = STAND STILL

"YELLOW!" = KEEP SNEAKING NEARER TO THE GOAL

"BLUE!" = THERE ARE HOT BUTTERED CHIMPS IN THESE WOODS

As soon as the captain of the Hiding Party thinks his teammates will be able to race to the home base safely, he shouts *"Run for Your Lives!"* This signal means that ALL of the people hiding should sprint to the home base. The game is won by the first member of either party who can reach the goal.

Should any member of the Search Party catch sight of an opposing player *before* the Hiding Party has started running for the goal, he shouts, "Run, Searchers, run!" Again, if a Searcher makes it back first, that team wins. (It is also possible to have the winning party be the one that gets ALL of its members to home base first.)

Shadow Tag

★ *4-PLUS PLAYERS*
★ *OUTDOORS*

This game of tag for younger players requires a sunny day. It is quite simple:

The player who is It tries to step or jump onto the shadow of some other player. If successful, he calls the name of the player, who then becomes It.

Children are not allowed to huddle together or inside of larger shadows; rather, they must seek open ground.

Smuggling the Geg

★ *8 TO 30 OR MORE PLAYERS*
★ *OUTDOORS*

This old Scottish game has its origins in smuggling. To begin, a Smugglers' Den of about 4 by 6 feet is marked in some central place.

The players are then divided into two parties, the Customs Agents and the Smugglers. Both parties agree on boundaries beyond which it is unfair to go, though the space available for play should be very large.

The Smugglers have the "*geg*." This is a small treasure, and should be an object easily handled, such as a pocketknife, key, marble, etc. One of the team members keeps the geg, but the identity of this particular Smuggler should remain unknown to the Customs Agents.

To begin play, the Customs Agents face inward and close their eyes in the Smugglers' Den. The Smugglers then run and hide in separate places. As the last of them reaches their final hiding places, the Smugglers give a call of "*Smugglers!*" This is the signal for the Customs Agents to begin the chase. ALL of the Agents must leave the Den, and none may remain behind to loiter near it.

The object of the Customs Agents is to catch the *one* player among the Smugglers who actually has the geg. The identity of this player relies on guesswork, so the Customs Agents will have to challenge *any* player whom they may find and catch. To do this, they must search for and then tag a Smuggler. Once a Smuggler is tagged, he must stop trying to escape. The Agent then demands, *"Give us the geg!"* Just like in real life, the Smuggler must truthfully confess and hand over the item if she has it.

If the geg Smuggler is caught, news of the discovery is shouted aloud, the Customs Agents win, and all of the players return to the Den and switch teams. If the player caught doesn't have the geg, she is allowed to go free.

But if the Smuggler holding the geg can safely return to the Den without being tagged by the Customs Agents, her team wins.

Of course, the Smugglers should try to engage the attention of the Customs Agents as much as possible with the players who do *not* hold the geg. Any distraction that holds the attention of the Customs Agents can be helpful for the real geg Smuggler.

Sprint 'n' Grab

★ *6-PLUS PLAYERS*
★ *PLAYGROUND, GYMNASIUM*

Not to overstate it, but this is one of the best chasing games in the history of . . . chasing games.

A goal is marked off across both ends of the play area. Midway between the goals, an object is placed. Any item will do, e.g., a glove, handkerchief, or Hello Kitty backpack. Heavier items, like stones, dumbbells, or oak trees may also be substituted. In line with the Item, a starting base is marked on each goal line (so two starting bases face each other).

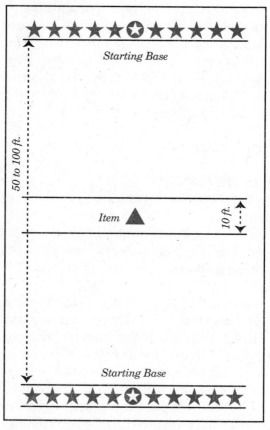

SPRINT 'N GRAB

The players are divided into two equal parties, each having a captain. Each party takes its place in one of the goals. The object of the game is for one of the runners to snatch the Item and return to his goal without the runner from the opposite goal tagging him. Both runners leave their starting bases at the same time on a signal.

Astute adults are encouraged to pick teams beforehand, keeping in mind the relative speed of the participants. The players can also be asked to choose a partner of their "speed"; these players would then run against each other.

The first runners run on a signal. If evenly matched, they may reach the Item together and go through many false moves and dodges before one snatches the Item and turns back to his goal. Should he succeed in reaching the goal before the other player can tag him, his team scores one point. Should he be tagged before he can return with his trophy, the opponent scores one point. The Item is replaced after each run. In either case, both players return to their original teams and go to the end of the line.

When each runner has run once, the teams exchange goals and run a second time. The team with the highest score at the end of the second round wins.

For large numbers of players there may be several Items, each having corresponding starting bases on the goals, so that several pairs of runners may compete at once. One Item for twenty players, ten on each side, is a good proportion.

The Squirrel and the Nut

★ *8-PLUS PLAYERS*
★ *GYMNASIUM*

Back in the misty dawn of time, before Head's Up, Seven Up had been invented, children used to play the Squirrel and the Nut.

This games works well in a classroom but can also work in a large room with the chairs for the players spread out in a circle. All of the players but one sit with heads bowed into the fold of their left arms as though sleeping, but each with a hand outstretched. The odd player, who is the Squirrel, carries a nut or other small object (like a geg!) and walks quietly through the aisles. At some point the Squirrel drops the nut into one of the waiting hands.

The player who gets the nut at once jumps up from his seat and chases the Squirrel, who is safe only when he reaches his nest . . . er, chair. Naturally, the other players wake up to watch the chase. (Care must be taken in the classroom that feet and backpacks are out of the aisles.)

Should the Squirrel be tagged before he reaches his nest, he must be Squirrel the second time. Otherwise the player who received the nut becomes the next Squirrel.

Stealth

★ 5-PLUS PLAYERS
★ PLAYGROUND, GYMNASIUM

As its name suggests, this game is unique in prizing subtlety over speed.

The playing area is marked off by two parallel lines that are anywhere from 50 to 200 feet apart. One player is chosen to be Counter, and stands on one of these lines with her back turned to the other players. They all line up on the opposite line.

The object of the game is for the players who are lined up in the rear to advance forward until they can be the first to cross the line where the Counter is stationed. But they may only advance by short stages, during which the player in front counts to ten.

The game starts by the Counter counting to ten loudly and rapidly. The other players move forward while she does this, but must stand still at the count of "ten." At this, the Counter turns quickly to look at them. The Counter will call the name of any player or players whom he sees moving. Any so called must go back to the starting line and start from there.

Players will learn to use much caution in moving forward, often stopping before the count of ten, to be sure that they shall not be caught in motion. Their progress may seem glacial, but this slower yet continuous method often works best.

This counting by the Counter and moving forward of the others continues until all have crossed the line where the Counter stands. The last one over changes places with him for the next game. It is also easy enough to have the players be on teams, with points allotted for first across, second across, and so forth.

Still Pond, No More Moving!

★ *5-PLUS PLAYERS AND A REFEREE*
★ *ANY LARGE OUTDOORS AREA*

After everyone washes their hands with soap, one player is blindfolded. The blindfolded player is then spun around four times by the referee so as to confuse his sense of direction. The others scatter during this, but upon the fourth turn, the referee says, *"Still pond; no more moving!"* whereupon the other players must stand still.

114

The blindfolded player begins to reach carefully about for another person. The players may resort to any reasonable devices for escaping the hands of the blindfolded person, such as stooping or dodging, so long as they do *not* move their feet.

When the blindfolded player finds someone, he must guess whom he has caught by touching the person's face and hair. He may not feel on the shoulders or around the neck. When caught, a player may try to disguise his identity by making himself shorter, etc., and, of course, players may choose to redirect the blindfolded player's hands if they're headed somewhere unfortunate.

If the blindfolded player correctly identifies the one before him, they exchange places. If incorrectly, the play is repeated.

The Third Man

★ *12-PLUS PLAYERS*
★ *PLAYGROUND, GYMNASIUM*

One player is designated the Runner and another the Chaser. All of the other players form two concentric circles (a double ring), with one player directly behind another and all facing inward.

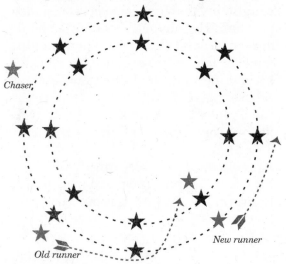

Chaser

Old runner

New runner

THE THIRD MAN

One way to achieve this formation is to have the players form a circle from a single file. Then have one player step in front of his neighbor on the right, and each alternate player in quick succession around the circle does the same. This brings all of the players into pairs, one behind another.

The Runner and the Chaser both start outside of the circle, one on one side of the circle and the other opposite. The object of the game is for the Chaser to tag the Runner. The Runner may save himself by stopping inside the circle and in front of one of the pairs.

By doing so, the Runner creates a "Third Man," namely, the outer player. This Third Man is now the new Runner and tries to evade the Chaser. He may seek refuge in the same way as before, but cannot take refuge in front of the couple immediately on his right or left. Should the Chaser ever tag the Runner, they exchange places. When the Runner becomes a Chaser, he can immediately start trying to tag the new Runner.

Great alertness is necessary on the part of anyone standing on the outside of a pair, as at any moment the Runner may take refuge in front of his row, making him the Third Man and liable to be tagged.

Both Runner and Chaser may dash through the circle but may not pause for a moment within the circle, except when the runner claims refuge in front of some couple.

VARIATION—To give the game more unpredictability, have the two players who form the circle stand face to face, with a distance of one step between them. The Runner now takes refuge *between* the two, with the one toward whom his back is turned being the new Third Man. This may be the person on the inside *or* outside of the circle!

Toilet Tag

★ *4-PLUS PLAYERS*
★ *OUTDOORS, GYMNASIUM*

Select a player to be the Plumber (you may choose to have more than one Plumber with large groups). While the other players scatter, the Plumber closes his eyes and counts to an arbitrary number like 17. Upon reaching said number, the Plumber begins trying to tag other players.

If a player is tagged, he impersonates a toilet by kneeling on *one* knee with one arm stuck out on the side. This player must stay frozen as a toilet until another player comes and sits on the his knee and pushes down on his arm while making a flushing sound. ("Whoosh" is a sensible choice.)

This flushing unfreezes the toilet player and both players are now free to escape the clutches of the Plumber. If a player is tagged twice by the Plumber, he or she becomes a Plumber also.

Play can continue until all players are frozen, or until a certain time limit is reached. The last player to be frozen or the last player left can be the Plumber for the next round.

Ultimate Frisbee

★ *6-PLUS PLAYERS*
★ *OUTDOORS FIELD*

This is a great game for exercise, and it's also very simple. To score, players just need to throw a Frisbee down the field to a teammate in the end zone.

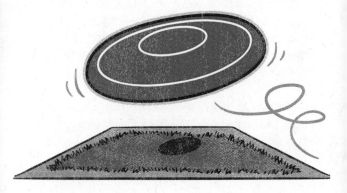

120

Decide on your field size based on how far your players can throw the Frisbee and by how many players there are. The playing field can be as large as 70 yards by 40 yards, or as short as 100 feet long and 80 feet wide. Be sure to have a deep end zone at each end, 20 yards deep (or more) if possible.

At the start of the game and after each score, both teams line up on the front of their end zone (or closer if you need to). The defense then throws the Frisbee to the offense.

The receiving team can let the Frisbee land and then pick it up, or they can catch it and start passing it downfield.

The offense moves the Frisbee *in any direction* on the field (including backwards) by completing a pass to a teammate. *Players may not run with the disc.* If they catch the Frisbee running, they should stop as soon as possible.

Rules of the Game

★ The person with the disc (the Thrower) has up to ten seconds to throw it. The defender guarding the Thrower can count out loud to ten if he/she likes. The defense gets the disc if the opposing Thrower doesn't throw in ten seconds.

★ The defender can try to block throws, but cannot touch the Thrower or the Frisbee as long as it's in the hand of the Thrower.

★ The Thrower can use a swivel or pivot foot, just like in basketball. If a pass is dropped or not completed (for example, it goes out of bounds or is blocked or intercepted), the defense takes the Frisbee and goes on offense.

★ *There is no physical contact allowed between players!* Picks and screens are not allowed. A foul occurs when contact is made. If a foul changes the possession of the Frisbee, then a foul is called and the Frisbee goes back to the other team.

The Five Rules of Frisbee[4]

1. The most powerful force in the world is that of a Frisbee trying to land under a car, just out of reach. (This is called "car suck.")

2. The better the catch, the higher the odds the person will then make a bad throw.

3. Never say "Watch this!" before doing something cool. Whatever you were going to do now won't work.

4. The best catches are never, ever seen. ("Did you see that? Anybody?")

5. In any group of people, someone will always say, "Hey, you could attach razor blades to the edge of this and have a cool weapon!"

4. Adapted from Dan "the Stork" Roddick's "The Ten Commandments of Frisbee."

★ Each time the offense completes a pass into the defense's end zone, the offense scores a point. They then line up at their end zone and pass it to the other team.

See which team can get to a certain score first, or play for a certain time period.

TIPS: There are no downs, like there are in football. There are no referees in real Ultimate Frisbee, so good sportsmanship is important. Respect the other players and have fun!

OTHER FRISBEE GAMES:

Decapitation!

★ *6-PLUS PLAYERS*
★ *OUTDOORS FIELD*

Two teams line up and face each other 15 yards apart. They take turns throwing the Frisbee as hard as they can at each other. Points are awarded for any catch made with *one* hand by the defense (point goes to defense), any drop or *two*-handed catch by the defense (point goes to offense), or any bad throw by the offense (point goes to defense.)

Boomerang Frisbee

★ *6-PLUS PLAYERS*
★ *OUTDOORS FIELD*

Players throw the Frisbee boomerang style and run to catch it themselves. The winner is the person who can throw and catch it while covering the most distance.

125

Frisbee Golf

★ *1 OR MORE PLAYERS*
★ *OUTDOORS*

It is easy to set up your own Frisbee Golf
Course. To do it, you need 5 to 9 hula hoops
or jump ropes. Just walk through a park
and set out your hula hoops or loop your
ropes to use as golf holes. Make some holes

shorter distances than others, and put some holes in challenging spots. To begin, just take your Frisbee and try to throw it into the hole. Keep track of your throws! (This is your score.) Once you succeed in reaching one hole, stand in that hoop to start throwing toward the next one.

Wink

★ *7 TO 25 PLAYERS*
★ *INDOORS*

An odd number of players are required for this game. One player is chosen to be It, and the rest are divided evenly between Sitters and Guards.

Enough chairs are placed in a circle to allow *one* chair to each *two* players and one for the odd player. (That is, one more than half as many chairs as there are players.)

A player sits in each chair, with all players facing inward. Behind each chair stands

127

a second player, who acts as a Guard. There should be one empty chair with a Guard behind it. This odd Guard winks at a Sitter, who at once tries to slip out of his chair without being tagged by *his* Guard and take his place in the empty chair. If tagged by his Guard before this happens, the Sitter must stay put.

The object of the Guards should be to avoid being the keeper of an empty chair, and therefore the one who has to wink. The Sitters try to evade the vigilance of the Guards by the quickness and unexpectedness of their movements. The Guards must keep their arms hanging at their sides until they see their Sitter has been winked at. They may not dash around the sides of the chairs that they guard, but must stay behind the chair at all times.

While Wink can be played with a time limit (with the "odd Guard out" losing), this is not necessary, as in and of itself the game is quite diverting.

Wolf

★ *5-PLUS PLAYERS*
★ *OUTDOORS*

This game differs from other hiding games as the searchers are the ones who flee for safety when the hider is discovered!

One player is chosen as the Wolf, who goes off and hides. The rest of the players are Sheep, with one of their number chosen as Shepherd. A place is chosen for a pen where the Sheep must stay and blind their eyes while the Wolf is hiding. The Shepherd counts to fifty and then the Sheep start out. They must all follow their leader, looking for the Wolf in each place where the Shepherd may search for him.

As soon as the Wolf is spied, the Sheep must stand still until the Wolf has taken a jump toward them. (The Wolf must do this *before* he may chase them.) Immediately after the Wolf has made his leap, the Sheep all turn and run for the sheep pen.

If the Wolf spies the Sheep *before* they spy him, and considers their position in relation to the sheep pen advantageous, he may call, "Stand your ground!" At this, the Sheep must instantly stand still and then take three steps toward the Wolf and stand again until he jumps toward them, when the chase for the sheep pen begins.

The Wolf may also run directly for the pen if he can reach it more directly than by chasing the Sheep. Should he reach the pen first, he may then tag the Sheep as they run in. One Sheep may act as a decoy to engage the attention of the Wolf while the others run into the pen.

Any Sheep tagged by the Wolf becomes a Wolf and joins the Wolf the next game, hiding either in the same den with him or in a separate den. When there is more than one Wolf, the Shepherd halts his Sheep whenever he spies *any* Wolf, whether it be the original Wolf or not, and all of the Wolves join in the chase when the Sheep run back to the pen. Traditionally, the game ends when all of the Sheep have been caught and converted to Wolfhood.[5]

Yards Off

★ *3-PLUS PLAYERS*
★ *OUTDOORS*

This is a New York hybrid of I Spy and Hide-and-Seek.

Two players are chosen—one to be It and one to be the Thrower. All the players stand grouped around a home base. The Thrower throws a stick or football (they don't roll much) as far away from the home base as he can. As soon as the stick touches the ground, the Thrower and all of the players (except for It) scatter and hide.

It then *walks* to the stick or ball, and brings it back to the home base. He then can

---

5. *As this is a rather dismal ending for the Sheep, innovative gamesters may wish to consider ways the Sheep can both retain their identity and win!*

begin hunting for the hidden players.

If It discovers another player, he must run back and touch the goal, shouting, "*One, two, three*, [insert name of player here]!" Anyone caught in this way becomes a prisoner at the home base unless he or she can beat It back to home base and shout, "One, two, three, *free!*" first. If successful, the player is free, and helps referee matters until the game's end.

At any time, a player who has *not* been detected by It may run in to Home Base and throw the stick away, at which point ALL of the prisoners become free and hide again. As before, It must *walk* to the stick, and bring it back to the home base again. Play then continues.

The game ends when all of the players have been freed or imprisoned in the home base. The last one caught becomes It for the next game.

Quiet Games

The games in this division are not necessarily silent, but they are distinguished by their lack of ring tone downloading, chasing, and other forms of vigorous exercise, and none require large play areas—in fact, almost anyplace will do.

Beast, Bird, or Fish?

★ *4-PLUS PLAYERS*
★ *ANYWHERE*

The players stand or can be seated, preferably in a circle. One player stands or sits in the center with a soft ball (not a softball). This player throws the ball to one of the players in the circle. The thrower says quickly, "Beast, bird, or fish!" then repeats one of these classes (e.g., "Beast, bird, or fish—BIRD!") and then counts to five.[1]

The player who has caught the ball must name some beast or bird or fish, according to the category last named. This must be done *before* the counter reaches five. For instance, the thrower will say as he throws, "Beast, bird, or fish— Bird! One, two, three, four, five," whereupon the other player must name a bird. This must not be a repetition of any bird previously named in the game. Should a player fail to meet these requirements, he changes places with the thrower.

Should he succeed, the thrower repeats the game by throwing the ball to some other player.

---

1. *An old English form of this game uses the words "Fire, air, and water." Players would name some animal that lives in the air or water when those elements were called out, but had to keep silent if "fire" was named.*

In the schoolroom this game may be played with all the players except the thrower in their accustomed seats. The categories can change depending on what is being studied that day.

Dumb Crambo

★ *4-PLUS PLAYERS*
★ *INDOORS*

The players are divided into two parties. One party leaves the room, and those remaining choose any *verb*, which is to be guessed by the outside party. The outside party is then brought back in and told some word that *rhymes* with the chosen verb. The outside party consult among themselves, decide on a verb that they think may be the right one, and without speaking, act out the word they have guessed.

The inside party must decide from this acting if the correct verb has been guessed. If not, they shake their heads.

If the outside party has guessed wrong, they retire and try another word, repeating this play until they hit upon the right word or until they give up.

If the party guessed right, they clap their hands and the two sides change places. No speaking is allowed on either side during this phase of the game.

Find the Ring

★ *5-PLUS PLAYERS*
★ *ANYWHERE*

The players sit in a circle, holding in their hands a long piece of string tied at the ends so as to form a circle large enough to go around to all. A small ring has been put upon this string before it was tied.

One player is chosen to stand in the center. The players who are seated then pass the ring from one to another, the object being for the player in the center to figure out who has the ring. The other

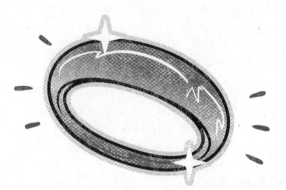

players will try to deceive her by making passes to indicate the passage of the ring when it really is not in their possession. When the player in the center thinks she knows who has the ring, she calls out the name of that player. If right, she sits down, and that player must take her place in the center.

This game may be played by the players repeating the following lines as the ring is passed around the circle:

ONE RING TO FOOL THEM ALL

SEE IF YOU CAN FIND IT

WE BOUGHT THIS RING AT THE MALL

BUT DON'T ASK US TO ADMIT IT

Outdoors, this game may also be played around a bush. In this case, the player who is It must circle around the outside of the ring formed by the other players instead of standing in the center.

I'm Going on a Trip

★ *3-PLUS PLAYERS*
★ *ANYWHERE*

This is a memory game that you may remember playing as a child. It can be played simply or at intermediate or very difficult levels, depending upon the players and their skill level.

LEVEL 1, one player begins by saying, "I'm

139

going on a trip to (here the player names a place) and I'm going to take (the player names any object)."

For example, let's pretend the first player says, "I'm going on a trip to the Moon and I'm going to take a pencil sharpener." The second player then repeats what the first player said and adds another item to be brought along, e.g., "I'm going on a trip to the Moon and I'm going to take a pencil sharpener and my mother."

The game continues in this fashion, going around the circle with the players repeating the string of items and adding another one to the list. Sooner or later, a player will be unable to remember the list correctly, at which point she or he drops out. Play continues until it comes down to the last person who can correctly recite all the items in the correct order. That person wins the game. For a prize, he or she gets a free trip to the Moon (and a free pencil sharpener!)

LEVEL 2: The take-along items named need to be appropriate for the trip or destination. For example, if the destination is the "Mountains," take-alongs should be things one could use or wear on the trip or at the destination—a tent, hiking boots, extra socks, a flashlight, toilet paper, a sleeping bag, etc.

LEVEL 3 CHALLENGE: Go crazy! Along with some easy-to-remember items, players occasionally name a take-along that's creative and laughable. See suggestions below. The crazier it gets, the shorter will be the game—because no one will be able to remember very many things! (This could be a fun way to wind down an otherwise lengthy Level 1 game and call it a night.)

Possible Trip Destinations (these are all real places)

Punkydoodles	Sopchoddy
Nimrod	Ouagadougou (*wah-ga-doog-oo*)
Flin Flon	Yeehaw
Woolloomooloo	Poopó
Weedpatch	Doostil
Affpuddle	Pukë
Djibouti (*je-boot-ee*)	Willacoochee

Vulcan	Mumbles
Booti Booti	Meeteetse
Wigtwizzle	Weeki Wachee

Odd Objects to Take Along

Antique cell phone	Nose-operated bicycle
Space rocks	Finger-paint brushes
Two-handled fork	Battery-operated comb
Bad medicine balls	Edible checkers
Ivy-covered tennis shoes	Ear wiper
Chocolate ray gun	Dangerous safety-pins

iPod People

★ *3-PLUS PLAYERS*
★ *INDOORS*

For this, you need someone with a good musical library on his or her iPod (which needs to be hooked up to speakers) or a computer.

Each player is given a slip of paper and pencil. The person controlling the iPod plays a tiny bit of a song, and each of the players writes on his slip of paper the name of the song and/or artist, or leaves a blank if she is unable to name it. The winner is the one who names the largest number of songs correctly.

After ten songs, the iPod controller backs up and reveals the identity of the tunes.

Astoundingly, this same process can also work live. Someone who knows how to play the kazoo, piano, or sousaphone can play brief bits of one song after another. This is an admirable game to use for old ballads, such as "My Old Kentucky Home," "Blue Bells of Scotland," "Orcs on My Trail," etc. In a company that is well up on current music, songs from popular operas and Broadway shows may be used successfully.

Kaleidoscope

★ 5-PLUS PLAYERS
★ ANYWHERE

This quiet memory game may be used with geography, history, literature, or any other subject.

The players are all seated, with the exception of three to six players who stand in a line in front of their fellows, each being given, or choosing, the name of a color— red, violet, green, etc. The players who are seated then close their eyes, and those who represent colors change places in the line. When they are rearranged, those who are seated open their eyes, and being called upon individually, try to name the colors in their new arrangement.

To add action, the colors can scatter and run around the room after being named, halting on a signal. The player who is to name them then runs around the room to the different ones as they stand scattered in this way, naming each as he reaches him.

Scat

★ *2 PLAYERS*
★ *ANYWHERE*

Players may choose to wear thin gloves for this game. One player holds on his upturned palm a ruler or a small thin strip of wood. The other player snatches this quickly and tries to "scat" or hit the opponent's palm with the ruler before he can withdraw his hand.

The game is made more interesting by fakes on the part of the player who has to take the ruler, giving several appearances of taking it before really doing so. When a player succeeds in hitting her opponent's hand with the ruler they change parts in the game. Count is kept of the unsuccessful hits, the player winning who has the smallest score when the play ends.

Up, Jenkins!

★ *6-PLUS PLAYERS*
★ *INDOORS*

This game is usually played with some sort of a time limit. The players are divided into two parties, and each party has a Captain.

The players gather around a table, one party on one side and the others opposite. A coin, usually a quarter, is passed from hand to hand under the table by one of the parties in an endeavor to conceal from the opponents which individual holds it.

After a reasonable time has passed to allow the one team to pass the coin, the

Captain of the opposite party calls, "Up, Jenkins!" At this point, all of the hands of his opponents are brought from under the table and held up, with palms up and fingers closed down tightly over the palms. (The quarter is hidden in one of these hands.)

The opponents may look at the hands from their side of the table in this way as long as they choose. The opposing Captain then commands "Down, Jenkins!" At this point, all the hands are slammed flat down simultaneously on the table (palms downward). This is done with enough noise to disguise the clink of the coin striking the table.

The object of the game is for the opponents (those not having the coin) to guess under which hand the coin is laid. The Captain of the guessing party alone calls for the lifting of one specified hand at a time, but his teammates must assist him with suggestions. The player named must lift the hand indicated, and that hand is thereafter to be taken from the table.

If the guessing party eliminates all of the empty hands so that the coin is left under the very last hand, they have won! The coin passes to them for the next round. If the coin is shown *before* the last hand is reached, the side holding it adds to its score the hands remaining on the table that were not ordered off.

Contests, Feats and Tussles

The following games make for an interesting and amusing change of pace from more traditional games, and often can be played between two people. The feats can be done solo and require only a small amount of skill, strength, or agility.

Boundary Tug

★ *2 PLAYERS*
★ *ANY LARGE ROOM OR OUTDOORS*

This game is a test of grip and balance.

Two lines are drawn or marked on the floor, 5 feet apart. Within this space, the two contestants face each other, with their right toes touching and each stepping backward in a strong stride position with the left foot. Both players grasp the end of a sturdy broomstick or wand at least a foot or more long (the longer the stick, the better it can be grasped with both hands). On a signal, each player tries to pull the other across one of the boundary lines.

As in a tug-of-war, the key to success is for the competitor to get his body low, and let the leg muscles do the work. This technique allows smaller competitors to overcome larger opponents.

To add a twist to the game, Boundary Tug can be played without allowing twisting or jerking of the stick. Advanced players may even want to try greasing the stick lightly with cooking oil to make it harder to grip. (At this point, the game should probably only be played outdoors!) And, of course, players may choose to play with their "off" hands (e.g., a right-handed player grips the stick with his left hand).

The Bump

★ *2 PLAYERS*
★ *ANYWHERE*

This was once an event at the Eskimo-Indian Olympics. It has two versions:

1. BACK BUMP: Two contestants stand back to back. Their feet should be a little more than shoulder-width apart. The players' heels should be no more than 2 inches apart, and they can be touching.

On the count of three, the two contestants try to make their opponent move one foot or both feet. The most obvious way to do this is to "bump" them (no hands or anything but the hindquarters can be used!). But players will quickly learn that moving out of the way of an opponent's bump can bring victory. Because of this strategy, contestants who *seem* mismatched by height or weight can often hold their own.

2. SIDE BUMP: Same rules as stated above, but in this case the players line up side by side. On the signal, they try to bump their opponent using only their hips. As before, any player who moves his foot or makes contact with anything but his hip is disqualified.

These games can also be scored, with points given to the winner of the matches.

Foam Noodle o' War

★ 2-PLUS PLAYERS (THE MORE, THE BETTER),
  1 REFEREE
★ ANY SOFT PLAYING AREA—WRESTLING MATS
  OR A GRASSY FIELD
★ FOAM NOODLE O' WAR, CONES OR OTHER
  MARKERS

Before you can *play* Foam Noodle o' War, first you have to *make* the Foam Noodle o' War. Here's how: Take an old bike tire and duct tape a number of foam swim noodles around it until it's completely covered.

Now get your kids together. If you have enough of them (say, nine or more), separate them into three or more teams and have them number off within their team. Place the Foam Noodle o' War at the center of your playing area. Teams should now spread out about 10 yards from the center of the playing area. Each team will have a "home cone" situated next to them.

The referee decides whether the kids will "combat (army) crawl" or race on all fours to the Foam Noodle o' War. Either way, the referee then calls a number. Players with this number race (either crawling or crabbing) to the Foam Noodle o' War and grab it. They then attempt to pull it over their cone, scoring a point. Of course, the other players will grab it and try to pull the Foam Noodle o' War to their cone, and a tug of war ensues.

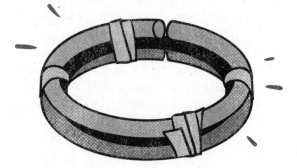

Players cannot impede each other's progress, nor can spectators assist. Body weight is not necessarily the deciding factor here; players who can get to the Foam Noodle o' War first have an advantage, as do those who keep their legs driving and their body weight low.

Harlequin Wrestle

★ *2 PLAYERS*
★ *ANY LARGE ROOM OR OUTDOORS*

This is a fun, nonviolent tussle. Each player stands on his or her left leg; the players then grasp right hands and each tries to make the other lower his upraised foot to the ground for balance, or to touch the floor with his free hand. A player may not touch his opponent with his own free hand to push him off balance.

Hopper Attack

★ 5 PLAYERS (MAY BE ADAPTED FOR 3-4
   PLAYERS)
★ OUTDOORS

A group of five players stands in a circle about 8 feet in diameter. One player is designated as the Enemy of the Hoppers, and the rest of the players are Hoppers.

The four Hoppers must fold their arms across the chest and hop on one foot. The object of the game is for the Hoppers to push the Enemy of the Hoppers out of the circle with their shoulders. Again, Hoppers may *not* use their hands. The Enemy of the Hoppers may stand on both feet and move around, but may not use his arms to ward off the Hoppers. He should avoid the Hoppers by running and dodging.

Should the Enemy be pushed out of the circle, the four Hoppers win. Should one of the Hoppers place both feet on the ground or unfold his arms, he must leave the circle, leaving the work to the other Hoppers. Players may want to have a time limit to avoid having one Hopper futilely chasing an Enemy for all eternity.

To play with fewer participants, the Hoppers may unfold one or both of their arms and use them in ousting the non-hopping opponent. (However, the Hoppers still must hop.)

I've Got Your Back

★ *2 PLAYERS*
★ *ANYWHERE*

Two persons sit on the floor back to back with arms locked, and retaining this position, they try to stand upright.

Motion Detector

★ *4-PLUS PLAYERS*
★ *ANYWHERE*

This is a game of subtle movement that requires keen powers of investigation. One contestant is chosen to be the Detective. The other players spread out at least an arm's distance away.

The Detective calls out, "Begin moving!" At this command, the other players start making mini-movements. These should be so small that they are not immediately apparent, but they must be *visible*. (Moving a tongue around in a closed mouth or gyrating one's pancreas doesn't count.) Admissible moves could be a tiny toe-tap, a miniscule muscle twitch, or an insignificant eyebrow alteration. Talented players will be able to wiggle ears or wag tails.

The object of the game is for the Detective to win points by correctly detecting the motion of as many players as possible in a single round.

The Detective is allowed one guess per person; if he guesses correctly, he scores a point. Play continues until everyone has had a chance to be Detective. The Detective with the highest score wins.

No Quarter

★ *SINGLE PLAYER OR 2 PLAYERS COMPETING*
★ *ANYWHERE AWAY FROM THINGS THAT BREAK*

The player raises one elbow level with the shoulder, the arm being bent to bring the hand toward the chest. Two quarters are then placed in a pile on the bent elbow. The player quickly drops her elbow and her hand moves downward in an effort to catch the coins before they fall to the ground.

161

Once the technique is mastered, players can compete to see who can grab the biggest stack of coins. As it is more difficult to balance piles of smaller coins, players should try the game with dimes, pennies, and euros.

Rooster Fight

★ *2 PLAYERS*
★ *OUTDOORS*

This is an old Greek game. (Apparently, the old Greeks had a sense of humor.)

A ring about 6 feet in diameter is drawn or laid out on the ground. The two players are placed in the ring. Each player then stoops and grasps his own ankles. (If the player is not this limber, he can grasp his calves.) In this position the players try to move each other by pushing with the shoulders. A player loses if he is knocked over, or loosens his grasp on his ankles, or is shouldered out of the ring.

Skin the Snake

★ 4-PLUS PLAYERS (BODY-CONSCIOUS TEENS
   AND 'TWEENS MAY PREFER TO OBSERVE
   FIRST)
★ OUTDOORS, GYMNASIUM

This game is very funny to watch, especially if done rapidly.

The players stand in a line, one behind another, with a short distance between them. Each player bends forward and

stretches one hand backward between his legs, while with the other hand he grasps the hand of the player in front, who has assumed the same position. Everyone will continue holding hands this way throughout the exercise.

When all are in position, the line begins "backing." That is, the player at the rear end of the line lies down on his back, and the player in front of him carefully walks backward over him. (This means that everyone in the line ahead must also move backwards.)

When the second-to-the-last player can go no farther, he also lies down, maintaining his hand holds and with the first player's head between his legs. This backing and lying down movement continues until all the players are lying in a straight line on the floor. Then the last one to lie down gets up and walks astride the line toward the front, raising the man next behind him to his feet, and so on until all are standing in the original position again.

Water Balloon Jousting

★ 2 KNIGHTS, 2 SQUIRES
★ BALLOONS, WATER, TWO BIKES, BIKE
  HELMETS
★ GRASSY FIELD

Jousting is the official game of Maryland, and in honor of the state whose motto is "Manly deeds, womanly words," we offer water balloon jousting. As you know, at jousting tournaments, knights ride on horseback at each other and try to hit their opponents with a long wooden spear. In this version of the game, two parties wheel their bikes at each other and try to hit their opponent with a water balloon.

Each knight and his squire should fill six water balloons. They set up their water balloons about 30 yards from the opponent. Each knight then takes one water balloon in hand. On a signal, they start riding towards each other. To avoid a head-on collision, the knights

165

bear right, staying to the right side of their opponent.

The knights try to go slowly enough to make an accurate throw when they are close enough. The rules can be agreed on beforehand. If both knights miss, then they both circle around and get new balloons. If one knight gets a hit, he can be declared the winner, and the knights can go back for another round. Or the squires can then get in on the action.

Beanbag AND Ball Games

The following games make for an interesting and amusing change of pace from more traditional games, and often can be played between two people. The feats can be done solo and require only a small amount of skill, strength, or agility.

Good Supplies to Have Around

1. *BEANBAGS, HACKY SACKS, AND/OR SMALL FOAM BALLS ARE USEFUL FOR A WIDE VARIETY OF TOSSING AND THROWING GAMES. THEY'RE ALSO GOOD TO USE INDOORS, WHERE THEY WREAK LESS HAVOC AND ARE MORE EASILY RECOVERED THAN REGULAR BALLS. AND THEY'RE ALSO PERFECT FOR KIDS LEARNING HOW TO JUGGLE!*

2. *SMALL CONES OR BOWLING PINS MAKE GOOD BORDERS AND LANDMARKS FOR GAMES, AND THEY ALSO CAN BE USED IN THE GAMES AS TARGETS.*

3. *GIANT INFLATABLE BALLS MAY NOT BE THE MOST PRACTICAL HOUSEHOLD TOYS, BUT THEY MAKE FOR EXTRAORDINARY FUN WITH A GROUP OF KIDS. IF THE BALL IS LIGHT ENOUGH, IT CAN BE HOISTED IN THE AIR FOR PONDEROUSLY SLOW VOLLEYBALL GAMES. DURABLE, HEAVIER BALLS CAN BE USED IN SOME OF THE GAMES DESCRIBED IN THIS CHAPTER.*

A Note on Throwing: A few of the following games involve one player throwing a ball at another in order to "get them out." Obviously, any ball used for this purpose needs to be made of light foam or soft materials. Furthermore, all throws must hit the other players below the neck; failure to do so results in disqualification for any game.

Finally, it's advisable to lecture players on the value of "not burning it in" (that is, throwing the ball as hard as possible). Not only is it unsporting, but the harder the thrower throws, the less control he has of the ball.

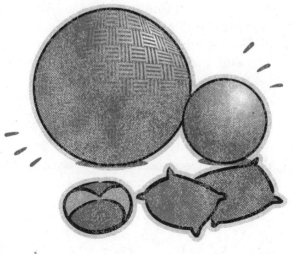

Ball Tag

★ *5-PLUS PLAYERS*
★ *PLAYGROUND, GYMNASIUM, SCHOOLROOM*
★ *FOAM BALL*

Each player chooses a "home." When played out-of-doors, trees may be used; indoors, the corners of a room could work. Players can run from one home to the next, but no more than one player can be safe at a home at one time.

One player is It and is given the ball. It must stay centrally located. The players at their homes signal to each other to exchange places, and as they run from one place to another, It tries to hit them with the ball. Anyone so hit changes places with the one who is It. All players assist in retrieving balls.

As in all ball games, the throw must not hit the other player above the neck or it doesn't count.

With lots of players playing, two or three players can be It, in which case there will be two or three balls that are in play at the same time.

Broom Balloon Ball

★ 8-PLUS KIDS, 1 REFEREE
★ GYMNASIUM, FIELD (ON A NON-WINDY DAY)
★ BALLOONS, 1 BROOM FOR EACH PLAYER

According to sports legend, this game was first developed at a witch's birthday party. There is no set field size for Broom Balloon Ball, so adjust your playing field's length according to the age and number of your players. However you set it up, you need two goals. This can be as elaborate as a portable soccer goal, or as simple as two trash cans about 6 feet apart.

Before game time, blow up a number of balloons. Do not use helium! Also, you will need as many brooms as there are contestants, which may take a bit of knocking on the neighbors' doors to rustle up.

Gather your players at midfield, and before you give them each a broom, explain very carefully that this is a non-contact sport and there absolutely cannot be any "high sticking." High sticking is what hockey players refer to as the lifting of any part of the hockey stick over shoulder height. In this case, the same principle applies to the brooms. Be sure to demonstrate to your players that the broom's brushes should be near or touching the floor at all times.

After dividing the players into two teams, have each team take a side of the field. Begin play by dropping a balloon into the middle of the field. Carefully monitor and interrupt play if necessary as you watch for high-sticking and potential dust-ups. The players then attempt to "sweep" and push the balloon through the opponent's goal. Introduce new balloons into play as old ones pop. Play can take place with two or more balloons.

NOTE: Helmets and eye protection are optional but encouraged. (After all, even if it's overkill, what's cuter than a bunch of helmeted, bespectacled kids chasing balloons with brooms?)

Clean Your Backyard!

★ *4-PLUS PLAYERS*
★ *GYM OR OUTDOORS*
★ *A WIDE ASSORTMENT OF ANY KIND OF BALLS*

This game will lead to short periods of frenzied activity, and may inculcate in children a willingness to clean up their rooms, albeit in a slipshod manner.

Divide the playing area into two separate but equal parts. Then randomly distribute an equal amount of balls on both sides. Any balls will do, though hard balls should be avoided. It's even more fun

if they're not all the same kind of balls.

Divide the group into two teams, and have one team take up residence on each side. The goal of the game is for each team to move as many of the balls as possible over to the other team's side of the field by the end of the allotted time. (This time can be as short as one minute.)

Have the players get ready, and then announce, "Clean your backyard!" The players can kick, throw, knee, head-butt, and otherwise propel the balls to the other side in any manner they see fit. But when time expires, an alarm must be sounded and play must stop. Score is kept according to how many balls are on each side at that time, with low score winning.

In a gymnasium, players will learn to not indiscriminately kick or throw balls, as these can bounce and roll back to their side. In an open field, players must again take some care, as balls only count if they are within the playing area's boundary.

Chuck and Run

★ *8-PLUS PLAYERS*
★ *ANY LARGE AREA*
★ *BEANBAGS OR SOFT BALLS*

The players are divided into two teams. The teams stand in two even rows, facing sideways. The players at either end step one long pace forward of the ranks, to the points marked 1 and 10 on the diagram. Player 1 has a beanbag and at the signal, he tosses the bag to

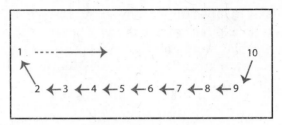

CHUCK AND RUN

Player 10 and runs toward the rear.

The line immediately moves forward one place, Player 2 stepping into the place vacated by Player 1. As soon as Player 10 has caught the bag, he takes his place in line with the rank and passes the bag to his next neighbor, Player 9. The bag is then passed rapidly up the line until it is received by Player 3, who tosses it to Player 2. Player 2, in his turn, as soon as he receives the bag, dashes for the rear, tossing the bag as he goes to the player standing at 10, who in this instance will be Player 1. The line again moves up, Player 3 now stepping out to the place marked 1. Confused? So am I, but it's actually very simple!

This play is continued until Player 1 is back in his original position. The rank that first gets the bag around to Player 1 after he returns to his original position wins!

Circle Stride Ball

★ *10-PLUS PLAYERS*
★ *PLAYGROUND, GYMNASIUM*

All but one of the players form a circle, standing with their feet spread out and touching those of adjacent players. This forms a permeable barricade for the ball that will be used in the game. (This can be a kickball, soccerball, basketball, or volleyball.)

The odd player stands in the center and tries to roll (not throw!) the ball outside of the circle by getting it between the feet of the players. Those in the circle try to prevent the passage of the ball, using only their hands. Once the center player succeeds in sending the ball through the circle, she changes places with the player between whose feet (or on whose right side) it passed. But if a circle player moves his feet in any way, he must change places with the center.

The center player should make lots of fakes and "no lookies," pretending to send the ball in one direction, and then turning suddenly and sending it in another.

For an extra challenge, when the ball has been sent out of the circle, the circle players can turn (facing outward) and then the center player tries to send the ball back inside according to the same rules.

Court Martial

★ 4-PLUS PLAYERS
★ PLAYGROUND, GYMNASIUM
★ ONE FOAM BALL OR BEANBAG, OR FOAM BALLS FOR ALL PLAYERS

All of the players gather within the

playing area, including one who holds the ball. On a signal, the ball man throws the ball as high as he can in the air. When that happens, all of the other players run in any direction as far as they can. The thrower remains on his place, catches the ball, and as he does so cries "Freeze!" Upon hearing this, all of the others must instantly stop running.

The thrower then aims his ball at one of these other players, and if he succeeds in hitting him, the player hit must change places with the thrower. Should he miss, all of the players return to the square and the same thrower makes another attempt.

Should he miss hitting a player a second time, there are two possibilities: 1) Play can continue until he does hit someone, or 2) He is "court martialed"; that is, the player stands 20 feet from the group with his back turned to them. These players are given foam balls, and on a signal, pelt him with their balls.

Curtain Ball

★ *4-PLUS PLAYERS AND A REFEREE OR SCOREKEEPER*
★ *GYMNASIUM, PLAYGROUND*
★ *VOLLEYBALL, BEACH BALL*

This is a great game, but its set-up is mildly peculiar. The playing area needs to be in a place where the two teams cannot see each other. Thus, a curtain hung over a volleyball net works, as does a high fence or hedge.

The game consists in hitting a ball backward and forward over the curtain or other barrier. The ball should not be allowed to touch the ground, and there is a score for the opponents whenever it does so. For large number of players, more than one ball may be used.

Players may try to deceive their opponents about where the ball is to cross the curtain. The more rapid the play, the more alert the players will have to be. The

great sport of the game consists in the
unexpectedness with which the ball may
appear at any given point. No outside
boundaries are necessary for this game.

Colossal Ball

★ *12-PLUS PLAYERS*
★ *BASEBALL FIELD OR OTHER OUTDOOR AREA*
★ *BEACH BALL, SOFT BAT, OR CHILDREN'S*
   FOAM SWIM NOODLE

Softball is a great sport, but it can be a little tough for younger players to join in on mixed-age games. Oh, the endless strikeouts! And rare is the six-year-old who can field a scorching grounder. ("Timmy? Can you hear me?")

For them, the game of Colossal Ball was developed. Teams are chosen and positions taken just as in softball. However, a beach ball is substituted for the softball. The batter can use a soft bat to hit it, or even better, a big foam swim noodle. (This is just one of the swim noodle's many non-aquatic uses.)

Because it can be a little too easy to catch flying beach balls for easy outs, one way to make it a little more challenging is to equip the fielders with hula hoops. If the fielders can manage to get the beach ball to go through the hula hoop before touching down, that would be considered an out.

Dead Center Ball

★ *8-PLUS PLAYERS*
★ *PLAYGROUND, GYMNASIUM*
★ *ANY REASONABLY SOFT BALL THAT THROWS WELL*

GROUND: The playing ground is marked out in one large square or rectangle. There should be a base or cone at each corner, with enough additional bases if needed along the boundary for half of the total playing group.

PLAYERS: The players are divided into two teams, with one team (called the Fringe Players) distributing its members at each base along the edge of the playing area. The other team (the Dead Centers) assembles in the center of the playing area.

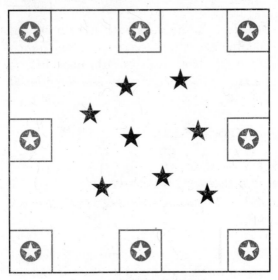

DEAD CENTER BALL

OBJECT: The chief object of the game is for the Fringe Players to suddenly throw the ball and hit one of the Dead Centers. Once hit, the object of any center player is to retaliate with the ball on any member of the Fringe Party. This is made more difficult by the fact that the Fringe Party will all turn and flee as soon as a Dead Center player is hit!

POINTS OF PLAY: The ball is started at any point among the Fringe Players. As they throw the ball amongst themselves, the Fringe Players try to mislead the Dead Centers as to their strategy, so the more rapidly the ball is kept in motion the better. As the ball moves about, the Dead Centers naturally move away from it.

There are no turnovers for bad passes, so it doesn't matter if their passes to each other are caught or not, nor if they bounce. But all passes from one Fringe Player party to another must follow the lines of the square and *not* its diagonals.

At some point, the Fringe Players try to take the Dead Centers unaware and throw the ball at one of them. Because of this, the Dead Center players should be scattered to diminish the chances of being hit by the ball. This means that the Dead Centers have to be alert and keep moving, even when the ball is not directed at them. The ball may be avoided by dodging, jumping, stooping, or any other maneuver *except* by leaving the playing area. There is no catching of the ball, as in Dodgeball, so Dead Centers must avoid the ball at all costs. (So all missed throws by Fringe Players are retrieved by Fringe Players.)

Whenever a Dead Center is hit, the Fringe Players are in danger of being hit in turn, and they must all run immediately in any direction to avoid this. A Dead Center who was hit picks up the ball as quickly as he can. Once he has possession of the ball, he calls *"Halt!"* At this, the fleeing runners must stand still, and the Dead Center player with the ball tries to hit one of them with it. This player can take one step with the ball from where he is standing and then throw.

SCORE—Sometimes keeping track of the score is merely distracting. This game can be played without scoring when any member of the Fringe Players who is hit by a Dead Center has to join the center team. The game ends when all of

the outer players have been so recruited.
Teams can then switch places.

If scoring is preferred, it can be done
according to whether the Dead Center
player hits or misses his opponent in this
throw of the ball after he has called a
halt. Every player who is hit scores one
for the Dead Centers. Every throw missed
scores one for the Fringe Players.

Deathball

★ 6-PLUS PLAYERS AND 1 OR MORE REFEREES
★ GYMNASIUM, A FIELD WITH BOUNDARIES
★ ABOUT 10 FOAM BALLS

*Because several balls are in play at once,
having more than one referee is a good
idea. This is one of the liveliest and most
interesting games around.*

Before play begins, about ten foam balls
are scattered in the middle of the playing
area.

Players can compete with a partner or on a team of 5 to 6 people. Players need to scatter around the room or field, touching the wall or toeing the boundary line.

Upon a signal, the players race to the foam balls in the center. While all players can run without a ball, once a player is holding a ball he *cannot move. The player has two choices. Within five seconds, he must either throw the ball to a teammate or* throw the ball and try to hit a competing player.

If the thrower succeeds in hitting another player, the "hit" player moves out of the field of play and into the Kill Zone, an out-of-bounds area. However, if the thrower hits any player above the neck, the thrower goes to the Kill Zone himself.

The winning team is the one with any players left after all other players are in the Kill Zone.

To keep play continuous: Once a player is sent to the Kill Zone himself, any players that he eliminated are released and can enter back into the game.

Dodgeball

This was already a well-established and popular game by the early 1900s. In addition to the universally known game, here are some worthy variations. As in traditional Dodgeball, having a referee is a good idea.

While there is an "official" dodgeball ball, any relatively soft ball that throws well will work. From 1 to 6 balls can be used for the following games.

Circle Dodgeball

★ *10-PLUS PLAYERS*
★ *PLAYGROUND, GYMNASIUM*
★ *DODGEBALL OR OTHER SOFT BALL*

The players are divided into two teams. One group forms a circle; the larger the circle, the more sport in the game.

The other group stands scattered about within the circle. The object of the game is for the Circle Players to hit the Center Players with a ball. (Surprise!)

As with other versions of dodgeball, the throws need to be below the neck, and a hit off a bounce does not count. Center Players must catch a thrown ball for it not to disqualify them. Any throws that hit a Center Player in the head (barring ones where the player stooped into it) don't count, and can disqualify the Circle Player from the match.

The Center Players may jump, stoop, or resort to any means of dodging except leaving the ring. They can dodge the ball, but they do not throw it at the Circle Players. But if they catch a ball, they can throw it over the heads of the Circle Players and force them to retrieve it.

Any player hit below the neck at once joins the Circle Players. The last player to remain in the center is considered the winner. The teams then change places for the next game.

Triple Dodgeball

★ *9-PLUS PLAYERS*
★ *PLAYGROUND, GYMNASIUM*

GROUND: The ground is divided into three equal courts about 30 feet long. Indoors, no out-of-bounds is necessary; outdoors, the field may also be 30 feet wide. The end courts may be shorter if full space is not available.

TEAMS: The players are divided into three equal teams, designated here as Red, White, and Blue. At the opening of the game, the two outer teams line up, each on its inner boundary line, each player standing with one foot on the line. The center team is grouped near the middle of the center court. The teams change courts at the end of each inning, and the formation just described is resumed as each inning starts.

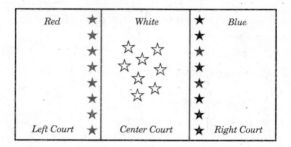

TRIPLE DODGEBALL

OBJECT OF THE GAME: The game consists of disqualifying opposing players by hitting them with a flying ball (not a bounce). The two end teams play against the center team, but *not* against each other. That means the center team can throw the ball back at either of the end teams.

START: The game is played in three innings, each of five or more minutes. The ball starts with the center team (the Whites, in the diagram). As play begins, one of the center players throws the ball at one of the opposing players (Red or Blue).

As the center players begin play, the Red and Blue players should run toward the rear of their courts. If the White player hits a player on the Red or Blue team, the hit player leaves the field and play continues.

Should the White player miss his opponents, the latter try to corral the ball before it rolls back into the center court. The player who gets it either runs up to the boundary line and throws at the Whites, or passes the ball to some

Inning	1	2	3	Total Lost Players
★ Red	0	3	7	10
☆ White	5	1	2	8
★ Blue	2	6	1	9

SCORECARD FOR TRIPLE DODGEBALL
WHITE TEAM WINS

other player of his own team who does this. The Whites naturally scatter to the farther boundary line of their court to avoid being hit. Should the ball fail to hit a White player, it is most likely to go entirely across to the Blue court, where one of the Blue team should catch it, and in turn try to hit the Whites.

To repeat, this is a game where the two ends play against the middle, but not against each other. A player in either of the end teams may be hit by a player on the center team, but it is not a part of the game for these end teams to try to hit each other. A ball thrown by either end team across the center court may be caught, however, by a player on the opposite end.

The referee blows his whistle whenever a player is hit so as to be out (i.e., hit by a ball "on the fly," not on a bounce) and also to stop play. If play is stopped, it always starts again with the middle team getting the ball. The referee also calls time for the close of innings.

POINTS OF PLAY: A player is not out if hit by a ball that rebounds, whether from the floor, another player, a wall, or any other object.

A player is not out if the thrower of the ball overstepped the boundary lines while throwing. The only kind of a hit that puts a player out is one from a ball "on the fly" thrown from behind a boundary line.

At the close of each inning (of five or more minutes) the teams change courts. In our example, the Blue team moves to the center, the White team to the left court, and the Red team to the right court. For the third inning another change is made in the same direction, so that each team will have played in each court.

SCORE: There are two different ways to score.

l. WHEN A NEW INNING IS STARTED AND THE TEAMS CHANGE COURTS, ALL PLAYERS WHO HAVE BEEN HIT AND ARE OUT RETURN TO THEIR TEAMS. EACH

INNING BEGINS, THEREFORE, WITH FULL TEAMS.

A SCORE IS MADE FOR EACH TEAM FOR EACH OF THE THREE INNINGS AND CONSISTS OF A COUNT OF THE PLAYERS WHO HAVE BEEN KNOCKED OUT DURING THE INNING. AT THE END OF THE GAME, THE TEAM WITH THE LOWEST SCORE WINS. WITH THIS VERSION, IT'S FUN TO POST THE SCORE AS THE GAME PROGRESSES.

2. *A SIMPLER WAY TO SCORE IS TO HAVE PLAYERS WHO ARE KNOCKED OUT STAY KNOCKED OUT. THE TEAM WITH THE MOST PLAYERS AT THE END OF REGULATION TIME WINS.*

GAME VARIATION: It is also possible to play Triple Dodgeball with eight or more players. The game is played by *two* opposing teams in a three-court field. One team takes its place in the center court, and the opposing team is equally divided, one half going to each of the end courts. The rules for play are exactly the same as for Triple Dodgeball.

Double-Death Corner Ball

★ *14-PLUS PLAYERS AND 1 OR MORE REFEREES*
★ *GYMNASIUM, PLAYGROUND*
★ *2 BASKETBALLS OR VOLLEYBALLS*

There are practically two games going on at once in DD Corner Ball. The game is usually played inside of time limits of about twenty minutes.

GROUND: The ground for this game should be outlined in a square measuring about 40 by 40 feet. In each of the four corners is marked a small goal, the two goals at one end belonging to one team and the two goals at the other end belonging to the other. Near the center are marked two small Bases.

TEAMS: Two teams are created, each one choosing its own Captain. The Captains select two Goal Keepers who are assigned to the two team goals. (Taller players with good jumping and/or catching ability are good choices for this position.)

197

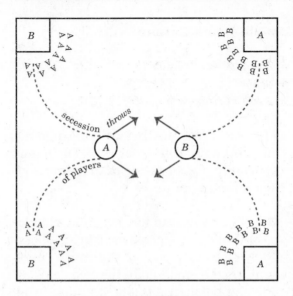

DOUBLE DEATH CORNER BALL

The remaining players are Guards. Each team divides its Guards into two parties, one for each of the opponents' corner goals. The best way to do this is to have the Captain line up his players. The players (including the Captain) then number off 1, 2, 3, 4, etc. "Odd numbers" are sent to guard one goal, and "evens" guard the other. Each guard should remember his number, as there is a constant rotation of players according to it.

OBJECTS OF THE GAME: The first object of the game is for a Guard on the Center Base to throw a ball to either of the corner Goal Keepers of his own team. Each ball caught by the Goal Keeper is a score.

The opposing Guards try to prevent the corner Goal Keepers from catching the ball. This is not just defensive play, as the Guards can also score. In fact, a Guard can score each time he catches a ball intended for the other team's Goal Keeper. That means that Guards should stay active and jumping as they try to catch the ball.

RULES AND POINTS OF PLAY: The game starts with the Number One Guard of each team standing in the center Base farthest from his goalkeepers' corners. The other Guards gather around the goals they are assigned to. The game opens with these two Guards throwing the ball to one of his team's two corners.

Each thrower has only one throw at a time. So after throwing the ball, the Number One Guard leaves the center Base, being replaced by the Number Two Guard. The Number One Guard joins the group of guards that Number Two just left. That means that the players must stay alert for turns and the Captain should call out numbers as play progresses.

The best kind of a throw to a Goal Keeper is a high curved ball that will go over the heads of the guards and fall within the goal. But *whoever* catches these thrown balls can earn points for his team. Touching the ball does not qualify as a score under any circumstances. It must be caught and held.

NOTE: During early rounds of this game, it is possible to let only balls caught by the Goal Keepers score. This simplifies matters until the players and referees get a sense of how the game's scoring and rotation work.

Caught or not, the thrown ball needs to be returned to the Center Base, where the next Guard prepares to throw it. Meanwhile, the same game is being played by the opposite team. That means that two balls are in play at once! This can make scoring challenging, which is why it helps to have more than one referee.

Goal Keepers and throwing Guards must keep both feet inside of their goals or bases. No Guard may step within the goal he guards.

Violation of these rules is a foul, and can score points for the opposing team.

Very alert and rapid play is needed to make this game a success. One team may play faster than the other, so it is *not* necessary that Number Six of the Red team and Number Six of the Blue team, for example, should be on the center throwing bases at the same time. The two games go on independently of each other.

Emperor Ball

★ *14 PLAYERS AND A REFEREE*
★ *PLAYGROUND, GYMNASIUM*
★ *BASKETBALL, VOLLEYBALL, NERF FOOTBALL*

PLAYING AREA: In the center of the playing area, three small circles are marked, forming the points of a triangle. These circles are called *bases*, and are about 15 feet from each other. The circles themselves are from 2 to 5 feet each in diameter.

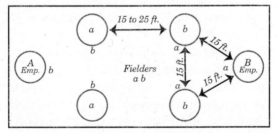

EMPEROR BALL

About 25 feet downfield is another triangle laid out exactly the same way, and the distance across the center of the field between the two inner circles of each triangle should be from 15 to 25 feet.

TEAMS: The players are divided into two teams (teams A and B in the diagram). Each team consists of One Emperor, two Basemen, three Guards, and one Fielder. Each Emperor stands at the farthest base. The two Basemen take up residence in the bases closest to their Emperor. Each team's Guards are stationed near each of its opponents' bases. Finally, the Fielders are assigned to the center of the ground, but they are free to run to any part of the ground. (The Fielders are also in charge of retrieving the ball if it goes out of bounds.)

OBJECT OF THE GAME: The object of the game is to have an Emperor score a point by catching a ball thrown by one of his Basemen. (Balls caught by the Emperor from the Guards or Fielder of his team do *not* count.)

Of course, the Guards from the opposing team try to prevent the ball being caught by an Emperor from one of his Basemen. For that matter, Guards and the Fielder will try to prevent ALL passes by the competition. After knocking down or intercepting a ball, the Guards or Fielder will try to throw it to their own Basemen or Fielder.

START: The referee makes sure all players are in position and ready, and then hands the ball to one of the Fielders (*which* one depends on the referee; it may be the winner of a coin toss, the shorter of the two, etc.). The ball is also put in play in this way after each point scored and after the ball goes out of bounds. (These balls go to the team that didn't throw it out of bounds in the first place.)

RULES: The Basemen may put one foot outside of their bases or circles, but at no time both feet. Each Guard must remain near the base he guards, but may not step within it even with one foot.

FOULS It is a foul to:

1. *BREAK THE RULES ABOVE.*

2. *SNATCH OR BAT THE BALL FROM AN OPPONENT'S HANDS.*

3. *TAKE MORE THAN TWO STEPS WITH THE BALL.*

4. *KICK THE BALL.*

5. *HAND THE BALL OFF INSTEAD OF THROWING IT.*

6. *HOLD THE BALL LONGER THAN TIME ENOUGH TO TURN ONCE AROUND QUICKLY (THREE SECONDS).*

If the referee calls a foul, the non-fouling team gets a free throw from one of their Basemen to their Emperor. That is, the Baseman's Guard cannot interfere, but the Emperor's Guard can still try to prevent the pass.

SCORE: A catch by an Emperor from one of his Basemen scores one point. Again, there is no score when the Emperor catches it from a guard or Fielder. Touching the ball is not enough for a catch: it must be caught in both hands. In case of dispute, the ball goes back to the last player who threw it. The ball is put back in play after every point scored, always going to the Fielder whose team was scored on.

The game can be played with time limits ranging from ten to thirty minutes. The time can be divided in halves, at which time players can rotate positions.

Human Arcade

★ *3-PLUS PLAYERS*
★ *INDOORS*
★ *SMALL FOAM BALLS*

We've all seen versions of the shooting gallery game in the arcade where targets pop up or run and it's up to the shooter to hit them before they disappear.

To play this version of the game, there needs to be a doorway opening into a hallway or big room with plenty of room on both sides of this opening. It's not a bad idea to pile up big pillows or even drag in a mattress so that each side of the doorway is padded.

One person is chosen to be the Target. The Target tries to move across the doorway without getting hit by the balls that will be thrown by the other members of the group. Where are they? These people are in whatever room looks in at the doorway, and they are ready to throw their foam balls. They can't be too close, though!

The Target can dive, run, crawl, or saunter across the doorway. He can also try to fake out the throwers and then go across. Rotating the Target can be done by having the first person to make a successful hit become the Target, or by waiting until the Target makes it across the doorway without being hit, and then choosing his replacement.

Overtake

★ *12-PLUS PLAYERS AND A REFEREE*
★ *2 BALLS OR BEANBAGS (PREFERABLY OF DIFFERENT COLORS)*
★ *GYMNASIUM, OUTDOORS*

This is a throwing game between a Captain and his team. These team members will be in a circle around their Captain, and ordered so that they are in alternating sequence with the players of the opposing team's members.

A referee should be on hand to start the game, keep score, and award points to the opposing team when fouls are made. The referee can also help with missed balls by tossing them to the Captain of the proper team.

FORMATION—The players are divided into two teams. If the different team members can be distinguished from each other in some way, all the better.

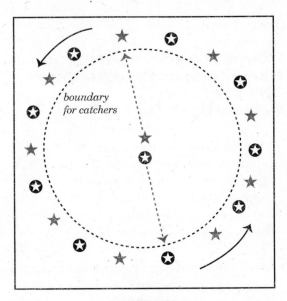

boundary for catchers

OVERTAKE

One player from each team is then chosen for Captain. The two captains stand in the center and start off back-to-back. The players of each team are then numbered consecutively. They take their places in a circle around the captains in such a way that the two Number One players are standing *opposite* each other. Next, the two Number Two players come out and stand to the right of their Number One opponents. Again, they should be facing opposite their numbered counterpart.

Keep in mind that as the circle is filled in, the players from each team should alternate, so that one would see a Team A player, then a Team B player, then a Team A player, etc.

The size of the circle may vary with the number of players and their skill in throwing to and catching from the Captain.

START: The objects of Overtake are 1) to complete the round of tossing and catching quicker than the opponents, and 2) to "overtake" the bag or ball which the opponents are tossing.

The game starts, on a signal from the referee, with the Captains standing back-to-back in the center, each facing the Number One player of his team. At the signal, each Captain tosses his ball to his Number One, who at once tosses it back to him. The Captain then tosses it to the next player of *his* team (the second player to Number One's right), and he tosses it back.

The two balls are thus being played around in the same direction, following each other; and one of the main features of the game is to have a ball "overtake" that of its opponents.

Play is continued around the entire circle until one of the captains tosses the ball back to his Number One. This is called getting the ball "home," and play then stops.

RULES AND POINTS OF PLAY: Players may stoop or jump to catch a low or high ball.

Players may lunge with one foot when tossing or catching with *one* foot, but moving both is a foul (unless the player is jumping up).

One or both hands may be used in tossing or catching.

A dropped ball is returned to play by the referee, who tosses it to the Captain.

The Captain needs good hands, so if a Captain drops a ball or bag three times, he changes places with his Number One; this Captain, failing three times, changes with Number Two, and so on.

No interfering with other players!

SCORE: It is possible to play the game without points; the team getting the ball home first winning. But if points are preferred, here are some scoring suggestions.

★ A ball that "overtakes" (passes) the opponents' ball scores five points.

★ The ball that gets back to its Number One (or "home") first scores four points.

213

★ Fouls (interfering with another player) score one point for the opponent.

★ The game is won on a score of ten points.

VARIATIONS: The game may be varied by requiring different methods of throwing and catching, such as catching with the right hand, left hand, both hands, etc. In the next inning or round the balls may follow in the opposite direction (to the left).

The balls can also go around twice, as opposed to once, or even five times. Each time the Captain receives the ball, he calls out a number corresponding to the number of times the ball has circulated, "One" for the first time, "Two" for the second, etc.

Paranoia Ball

★ 6-PLUS PLAYERS AND 1 OR 2 REFEREES
★ GYMNASIUM, A FIELD WITH BOUNDARIES
★ 8 TO 10 FOAM BALLS, 1 LIGHTWEIGHT CONE
  OR PIN PER TEAM

Because several balls are in play at once, having two referees is a good idea.

As with Deathball, eight to ten foam balls are scattered in the middle of the playing area. Players can compete individually or on teams of three.

Unlike Deathball, each team tries to protect their cone or pin. The players set up their cone somewhere in the room or on the field, at least 6 feet from the walls or boundaries. The players stay near their cones.

Upon a signal, players can race to the foam balls in the center. As before, once a player is holding a ball he *cannot move. He must either throw the ball to a teammate* or *throw the ball and try to knock over the cone of a competing team*. His teammates may try to move to a good spot on the floor and get a pass. Balls can be thrown against the wall behind the cones or off of the legs of defenders, so that they bounce off and knock the clubs down.

Cone defenders may try to block shots, but they cannot touch their own cone in any way. Any part of the body can be used to block a shot, but the defender must remain standing and the thrower may not be touched. A cone defender can also throw a ball, provided he doesn't move with the ball once he has it.

Teams may want to send one player out to throw balls while at least one player stays behind to protect the cone. If a team's cone is knocked over by a ball OR if a defender accidentally knocks his own cone, his whole team is eliminated. Play continues until one team is left.

For continuous play, eliminated teams

can go back into action once the team that vanquished them is likewise eliminated.

Pig Ball (aka Sweat Ball)

★ 6-PLUS PLAYERS, 1 REFEREE
★ GYMNASIUM
★ FOOTBALL (PREFERABLY NERF), BASKETBALL HOOP

Pig Ball doesn't have a very attractive name, but people who play this game love it. The playing field is a basketball court, and while half-court works, the full-court version gives a better workout.

To start, two equal teams are formed. These teams can have as few as three or as many as eight players, but five is best.

A team scores by making a basket with a football. To do this, one team inbounds the ball in the same way they would if they were playing basketball. But that's

where the similarity ends. First of all, it's more fun if this game is played with no out-of-bounds. So players can move anywhere they want!

Second, since it's impossible to dribble a football, the ball has to be brought upcourt with passing and catching.

Pig Ball is very similar to Ultimate Frisbee (see p. 120) in these ways:

★ There is no backcourt rule, and the ball can be moved in any direction.

★ A dropped, tipped, or otherwise incomplete pass means a turnover.

★ A defender can guard anyone passing the ball, but he can't touch the passer or knock the ball out of his hand. No physical contact is allowed on the receivers either!

★ After a caught pass, the catcher must stop as soon as possible. From that position, he can throw or shoot the ball using one foot as a pivot foot. He can only hold onto the ball for five seconds; a defender can call out a count out if he wants. ("Five! Four! Three! Two! One! Pass!")

When a player "shoots" the ball at the basket, one of three things can happen:

1. *THE BALL GOES THROUGH THE HOOP. SCORE! NOW THE OPPOSING TEAM TAKES THE BALL OUT UNDER THE BASKET.*

2. *THE SHOT HITS THE BACKBOARD AND MISSES. THE REBOUND IS NOW UP FOR GRABS! IF THE TEAM ON*

OFFENSE GETS IT, THEY CAN SHOOT OR PASS. IF THE DEFENDING TEAM GETS IT, THEY BRING THE BALL UPCOURT.

3. *THE BALL COMPLETELY MISSES THE BACKBOARD AND THE RIM. THIS IS CONSIDERED AN INCOMPLETE PASS AND IS AUTOMATICALLY A TURNOVER.*

To make sure that everyone is getting a chance to play, the referee can insist that the same player can't make two baskets in a row.

Rounders

★ *8-30 PLUS PLAYERS AND 1 OR MORE REFEREES*
★ *GYMNASIUM OR ANY FIELD*
★ *1 NERF FOOTBALL AND 1 BAT*

It's best to play this game with at least one King. The King is an adult or other respected person who is the referee.

The game goes especially well with immense groups of people.

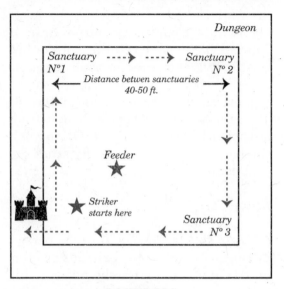

ROUNDERS

Rounders has been around for centuries, and it has taken its place as one of the finest games of all time. It has influenced the modern games of baseball, cricket, and Death Match 3000.

In Rounders, there is a player called the Striker. He hits the ball and starts to run. He wants to score! Each time any Striker successfully completes a journey *around* the *Sanctuaries* and returns to his or her Castle, that is a score for their team. At the end of the game, the team with the highest tally (the most runs scored) wins. The only way to prevent a Striker from scoring is to "peg" him or her OR to catch the ball they strike on the fly or on the first bounce.

Rules

1. INFINITE SWINGS. The *Striker* (the person hitting or *"striking"* the ball) has no limit on the number of tries she needs to hit the ball. There is no striking out. The Striker keeps trying until the ball comes in contact with the stick. (The Striker must take an actual *swing* at the ball.)

2. THE BALL MUST BE FED WHERE STRIKER WISHES. The *Feeder* is the person from the other team who throws (or *"feeds"*) the ball to the Striker. The Feeder must throw the ball where the Striker wants it. If the Striker is unhappy with a Feeder, the

Striker asks for a new Feeder from the other team. The Feeder should try to give the Striker a good throw; no rolling the ball or burning it in. (The Feeder doesn't have to worry about someone "stealing a base." You can't do this in Rounders.)

3. RUN ON ANY HIT. Any time the stick hits the ball, (unless it's a "tip" that does not make any forward progress), it is a hit and the Striker *must* run. The ball may be struck anywhere. There are no out-of-bounds! The Striker can also run anywhere. (See FAQs, page 226)

Important: Any Strikers already at the Sanctuaries DO NOT have to begin running when the ball is struck. (There is NO need to tag-up, like in baseball on fly balls.) However, once they begin to run, THEY HAVE TO KEEP GOING at least to the next Sanctuary.

4. RUN CLOCKWISE. Upon hitting the ball, the Striker then must run *clockwise* around the Sanctuaries. The Striker does not need to touch any of the Sanctuaries and may run *anywhere* on the field as long as she eventually passes *outside* or *around* each Sanctuary. (That's why they call it *Rounders!)*

5. STRIKER IS OUT. The Striker is out if the hit is caught in the air OR after the first bounce. Also, any Striker is out if he is *plugged* (hit with a thrown ball) while running. He is *not* out if he is on or holding a Sanctuary (one that he hasn't used before—see Rule 7) before he is plugged.

A note on plugging: The throw MUST HIT THE STRIKER BELOW THE NECK. If it doesn't, the Thrower goes to the Dungeon.

6. SANCTUARIES ONLY WORK ONCE. Once a Striker has touched a Sanctuary, she may not let go of it and then grasp it again—it has been *used up* for that Striker. More than one Striker can use a Sanctuary at once; one Striker can pass other Strikers up as he runs.

7. NO BLOCKADES. No defending team member may touch or get in the way of a Striker in an attempt to prevent him from getting to a Sanctuary or going around the Sanctuaries.

8. FREEZING PLAY. If the Feeder gets the ball in the pitching area and touches the ball to the ground while yelling, *"Freeze!"* then the Strikers on the field must go to the closest sanctuary that they haven't used yet and hold play.

9. EVERYBODY OUT. The teams change sides when the Castle's team has gone through their *whole* Striking line-up. That means that every person on that team has either scored or gotten out. *Strikers may not be stranded on Sanctuary.* Play continues *until the last person in the line-up is either out or scores.* (Subsequent Strikers who already batted *can* be stranded.)

10. MASTER ROUNDER. The last Striker *can become a MASTER ROUNDER* if he decides to try to circle the bases twice.

After leaving the Third Sanctuary after his first trip around, he may try to make the full trip around again without stopping and get back to the Castle. If he makes it, his whole side gets to bat again; if not, the inning is over and the other team comes up. (You might want to keep your fastest person till last because of this!)

11. THE DUNGEON. Any Defender who plugs a Striker above the neck, or blocks a Striker's route, goes to the Dungeon. (This is like a penalty box.) Any bad sports go to the Dungeon as well!

12. THE KING IS ALWAYS RIGHT! Once the action gets going, it can be almost impossible for the King to see the whole playing field. It doesn't matter: *the King is always right!*

Frequently Asked Questions

QUESTION: What if I think the King is wrong?

ANSWER: See rule number 12.

QUESTION: The Striker hits the ball toward a Defender near the first Sanctuary. The Striker then runs away. Is this legal?

ANSWER: It's not only legal, it's smart. The Striker would get pegged if he ran toward the player with the ball! If he runs away, he has a much better chance; of course, he will need to *eventually* run back to the first Sanctuary and stay there or go around it.

QUESTION: A Striker runs *around* all the Sanctuaries without touching them, gets confused, runs to Sanctuary Two and holds it. Is this legal?

ANSWER: Actually, it is legal. The Sanctuary hasn't been "used up" for him because he never touched it.

QUESTION: A Defender tries to "peg" a Striker. The ball bounces and then hits the Striker. Is the Striker out?

ANSWER: No. The ball must be "on the fly," not "on the bounce" when it hits the Striker.

QUESTION: A Striker is being chased by someone with the ball. The defender tries to peg the Striker, but the Striker ducks, which results in the Striker being hit in the head with the ball. What is the decision?

ANSWER: The Striker is out; there is no penalty.

Silent Ball

★ *5-PLUS PLAYERS AND A REFEREE*
★ *LARGE ROOM OR CLASSROOM*
★ *NEWSPAPER AND MASKING TAPE*

This excellent game's ball needs to be prepared beforehand. Masking tape and newspaper are needed. (Trust me.) Take the front page off of a full-size newspaper (no tabloids) and crumple it loosely into a large ball. Now take the masking tape;

attach one end of the tape to the ball and begin rolling the tape around and around without squishing the newspaper down too much. Once all the newspaper is covered with tape, make one more ball!

They will fly well, but because they're light, the Silent Balls will not injure anyone who is hit with them.

229

The group of players should be arranged around the borders of the room. They should be at least an arm's length away from each other. Play begins with the referee silently handing a ball to a player. The player then throws the ball to another player. *Unlike* most games, the other doesn't need to be watching for the throw. It's best to throw to someone who isn't expecting it! Thus, quick throws and "no lookie" passes are encouraged.

Throwers should imagine that everyone is wearing a jersey with a number on the chest, and then throw at the imaginary number. A "good throw" is defined as one that hits (or nearly hits) the other player's number. If a player drops a good throw, or doesn't make a genuine attempt to catch a decent throw, the player is eliminated.

If a thrower makes a bad throw that is *not* caught, the thrower is eliminated. Many times, the thrower will make a bad throw that is caught anyway, so play continues.

With a large group, two Silent Balls can be used. (The second ball is usually secretly introduced into play after a minute or so by the referee.)

Rules:

★ No holding the Silent Ball for more than four seconds.

★ No burning it in.

★ Any throw made to a player to the direct left or right of the thrower must be made underhand.

★ No throwing it back to the person who threw it to you (until the final Duel).

★ No noise or complaining about the referee's decisions.

★ As always, no throws that hit the other player above the neck.

When everyone is eliminated but the last

four players, the four should spread out. Two of them get balls, and the referee says "Clockwise!" (or "Counterclockwise!"). The players then throw the balls in that direction as quickly as possible until there are only two players left.

Then the winner is decided by Duel. Each player gets a ball. On a signal, they quickly throw the ball to their opponent. As before, the throws have to be good, or they are eliminated. The first player to drop a ball or make a bad throw that isn't caught comes in second.

NOTE: Silent Ball can also be played without the silence, in which case it becomes "Laugh and Yell Ball."

Simian in the Center

★ *5-PLUS PLAYERS*
★ *GYMNASIUM, PLAYGROUND*
★ *BASKETBALL OR VOLLEYBALL*

All of the players (but one!) form a circle,

with 6 to 8 feet between players. The odd player is the Simian. He stands in their center, holding a basketball or volleyball.

Play starts with the Simian tossing the ball to *any* player in the circle, and immediately running away outside the circle.

The player to whom the ball is thrown must catch the ball (if he drops it, he retrieves it), place the ball on the ground in the center of the circle, and at once chase the Simian. The Simian then tries to get back to the center of the circle and touch the ball before he can be tagged. Should the Simian succeed in this, he joins the circle, and the other player becomes the new Simian, who throws the ball for the next round. If the first Simian is tagged before returning to the ball, he throws again, and the one who chased him returns to the circle.

Spud!

★ 5-PLUS PLAYERS
★ GYMNASIUM, PLAYGROUND
★ ANY SOFT BALL OR BEANBAG

For this popular game, the players stand in a loose group, with one player in the center holding the ball at shoulder height. The center player drops the ball, at the same time calling the name of one of the other players. All players except the one called immediately scatter as far as possible, as they are liable to be tagged with the ball.

The player called secures the ball as quickly as possible, and tries to hit one of the other players with it. He may not run to do this, but must stand at the spot where he picked up the ball.

If he misses hitting another with the ball, it is called a "spud." The other players are encouraged to shout "Spud!" as the thrower chases the ball down again, stands where he gets it, and tries again. The other players naturally flee from him as before.

If and when the thrower hits a player, the other players shout "Spud Master!" The player who was last hit with the ball is now the one who has to get the ball and try to hit someone else with it. Thus the game continues.

EARLY 20TH-CENTURY RULES: Whenever a thrower gets a spud (by virtue of a missed throw), it counts as one point against him. When any player has three spuds against him, he must stand 20 feet from the other players, with his back to them, and they each have one shot at him with the ball. The spud-offending victim then starts the play again from the center of the ground.

Team Handball

★ 8-14 PLAYERS, 1 REFEREE
★ BASKETBALL COURT OR SIMILAR-SIZED OUTDOOR FIELD
★ TWO GOALS, ONE BALL THE SIZE OF A CANTALOUPE (NERF BALL OR SLIGHTLY SOFT VOLLEYBALL)

Team Handball is not like the handball game that's played off the wall. This is very close to the Olympic Team Handball event, except this is a non-contact version. It is usually played with two teams of seven players (6 court players and a goalie), but it is possible to play with fewer players.

The object of the game is to throw the ball past a goalkeeper and into the opponent's goal (the goal itself should be about 3 yards wide and 2 yards high). That means that a goal area needs to be marked off at each end of the court. If a basketball court is being used, the width of the key is the width of the goal. Otherwise, mark off a

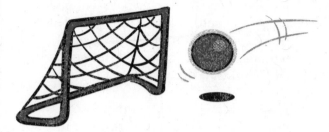

half-circle about 6 yards in front of the goal for the goalie to occupy. The goalie is the ONLY player allowed in the goal area; his team's defenders can line up around the goal, but they cannot go into the goalie's area.

To start play, have a coin flip to decide which team gets the ball first. The ball goes to the winning goalkeeper, who starts the game by passing the ball to one of his players.

The players can move the ball down the court by either dribbling or passing it to teammates, but passing is the more encouraged option. Dribbling is useful

237

for getting into a better position to pass. Players should not hold the ball for more than five seconds. If a pass goes out of bounds, the ball is passed in-bounds by the team that didn't touch it last.

Again, this is a non-contact game, and players are not allowed to pull, hit, or punch the ball out of the opponent's hands. Instead, they should play defense as they would in Pig Ball or Ultimate Frisbee.

Referees can award free throws in the event of minor fouls. Team Handball can be played to a certain score, or for time limits.

Telepathy Ball

★ *4-12 CHILDREN, EACH WITH A MATCHING ADULT*
★ *BASKETBALL COURT*
★ *BASKETBALL*

While "helicopter parents" didn't exist in the early twentieth century when this

game originated, Telepathy Ball gives adults a great chance to keep very close tabs on their kids while they play.

Telepathy Ball begins by having the kids divide into two basketball teams. A parent stands behind each player and holds onto the back of the child's waistband with at least one hand. Then play begins.

Because basketball is a game full of

unexpected twists, jumps, and turns, the adults will be hard-pressed to keep up with their players. However, if the parent has been observing his or her child in sports, he or she *should* have the ability to anticipate where his or her player will go, based on the game's action.

Adults who are successful at these predictions will find that they are not slowing their children down much, while more out-of-the-loop parents will find themselves playing Parasite Ball as opposed to the more advanced Telepathy Ball.

Accomplished Telepathy Ball pairs can then try the most advanced test of their mind-body link: Soccer!

I. Types of Games

II. Number of Players

10 PLUS PLAYERS

III. Playing Area

INDOORS, LIVING ROOM OR GAME ROOM

NOTE: Games that can be played indoors in a living room or game room could easily be played in a small area of a gymnasium or outdoors.

IV. Age Group

FOR PRESCHOOLERS

FOR SCHOOL-AGE CHILDREN, 6–18

SUITABLE FOR ADULTS AS WELL AS CHILDREN